NOT YOUR AVERAGE **5K**

Jill Angie has created a 5K training plan that not only gets you to the finish line but addresses the #1 reason that many new (and experienced) runners face when taking on new challenges. Mindset. In this easy to follow program, Jill walks you through exactly what to do, when to do it, and how to get rid of self-doubt, fear and anxiety known as your "inner mean girl" so that you finish strong, confident, and proud. Whether you struggle with the physical aspects, mental aspects, both or neither, this guide will have you totally prepared on race day.

STEVE CARMICHAEL
Running coach and host of The RunBuzz podcast,
www.RunBuzz.com

Not Your Average 5K is a highly readable and engaging book that will have you BELIEVING you can do a 5K in eight weeks and provides a roadmap with plans to accomplish it. It is authentic, thorough, and motivational from start to finish! We highly recommend this book for anyone wanting to do their first 5K.

ADAM GOUCHER AND TIM CATALANO
Of Run The Edge, www.RunTheEdge.com

This book is perfect for anyone who is nervous about trying their first race. Jill brings not only certified running coach expertise, but her own personal experiences as a "not your average" runner who isn't a 6-minute mile, 0% body fat, constant gym rat that you can't relate to. This book and training plan give you EVERYTHING you need to get ready—physically and mentally—to conquer your first 5K, It's practical and encouraging while staying lighthearted and real. Running is more mental than physical—you CAN do this, and Jill is with you every step to keep you comfortable and confident.

DANA AYERS
Author, *Confessions of an Unlikely Runner (A Guide to Racing and Obstacle Courses for the Averagely Fit and Halfway Dedicated)*, DCDana.com

Jill Angie leaves no stone unturned in this full and frank book. Becoming a runner is about overcoming obstacles that you build yourself, it's not just about putting one step in front of the other. Jill has created the ultimate resource for anyone who wants to run but thinks it's too hard. I'm sure there will be a lot more runners as a result of this. Reading it brought back all the barriers I built for myself when I decided I wanted to change my life through running. I wish I'd had a copy of this book back then, as it took many attempts (over a couple of years) to make a breakthrough. Running is a central part of my life now and I couldn't imagine a life without it. If you want to change your life but you don't know how to start, you need to read this book.

ALISON KING
Founder and coach at Run For Your Life Coaching,
www.runforyourlifecoaching.co.nz

Jill has brought us another hit. *Not Your Average 5K* gets you the tools you need to make your dream a reality. As a fellow blogger, one of the most frustrating comments I get is: "I'd like to ____ but..." In my opinion: "But, whatever!" Jill talks you through those "buts" and helps define a plan for success. She verbalizes those excuses for you so you can work right past them and succeed. You aren't too fat, too out of shape or too busy to do a 5k. Now get those shoes ready and I'll see you at the finish line!

LAURA BACKUS
www.FatGirlIronmanJourney.com

Many moons ago, I directed an annual series of 100 women's 5K races nationwide for the Road Runners Club of America. At the time, women's running clothes were a new concept and we were still underrepresented in the running world. The Women's Distance Festival was founded to protest the lack of distance running events for women and then evolved to encourage women runners by helping them train for their first 5K. Fast forward 25+ years and you find Jill Angie carrying the running torch. *Running with Curves* proved there is no such thing as a "typical" runner and now *Not Your Average 5K* follows up, supporting the fact with a practical plan, actionable advice and motivation aplenty.

Yes, we can all be runners especially with this book, which helps you commit to the dream of running a 5K, breaks it down into achievable goals and then helps you overcome the resistance all runners (yes, even champions) encounter. Download today and you'll be celebrating finishing your first 5K in just a couple of months! (And blowing raspberries at the naysayers who said you couldn't!)

LISA CULHANE

Transition Coach and bestselling author of *"Discover the New G Spot (Or How to Unfriend Your Guilt)"*, www.lisaculhane.com

WHAT READERS LIKE YOU ARE SAYING

As a women's self-image coach and brain retraining expert, I always recommend my clients get out of their comfort zone and do something that feels impossible—when they accomplish it, the smile on their faces, that feeling of triumph, makes every bit of work worth it.

Jill Angie has taken what feels like "impossible" to so many— to run a 5k—and brought it into the realm of "possible" by breaking down the process from start to finish....and when I say "start" I mean literally, from you sitting on the couch, thinking about making a better choice for your health...to finish, including what exactly you can expect on race day... and beyond.

EVERYTHING you need to know is in this book. Whether you want to try something new, add regular exercise in to your week, or to become an avid runner. And the most beautiful part: Jill has written her soul into this book. She has made the entire process non-scary, and included topics like what to wear, how to start, what to do if you forget your mp3 player—seriously practical advice.

Perhaps the most important? She talks directly to you, and helps you settle down that inner mean girl that says you can't do this. She tackles the head voices straight on, helps you step right past obstacles, and cheers for you to finish. Let yourself experience triumph: read this book, and get started on a new life today!

LISA D'ALESSIO
Body Mentor, Intuitive Healer, Writer, Speaker, Brain Geek, www.lisadalessio.com

---

Jill Angie has done it again. I read her first book, *Running with Curves,* and refer to it all the time. But after reading *Not Your Average 5K, A Practical 8-week Training Plan For Beginning Runners*, I never realized how much I really didn't know. She writes as if she is speaking directly at you adding her comical style. But she goes deeper than the average step by step running book. She teaches us to understand the psychological effects running has on all of us and teaches us how to handle all obstacles. I highly recommend this book to anyone who wants to understand the difference between running and becoming a runner.

PINKY LOVE

Not Your Average 5K is not your momma's fitness how-to guide! Discover how to get started with running in a humorous and approachable way that will have you laughing and nodding along in empathy! Have you ever tried a "beginner" fitness program only to find that you just can't cut it and subsequently head right back to the couch? Defeating, right? *Not Your Average 5K* presents a beginner guide to running that is *actually* achievable by a normal, average person: you!

You CAN run a 5K, no matter your size or current fitness level, and *Not Your Average 5K* is the guidebook that will get you there. The book leads you through a personalized training program based on your fitness level through the lens of two different "real-life not your average" runners: Cindy and Sarah.

Author Jill Angie provides not only a comprehensive set of instructions for training for your first 5K, but phenomenal cheer-leading and support that will help you stick with running as a new healthy hobby. Are you ready to be *Not Your Average Runner?* What are you waiting for? NOW is your time!"

VICTORIA NESTI

If you're like me, you grew up hating running or afraid to run, mostly because the *they*s of the world told you that you shouldn't or couldn't. Jill Angie absolutely proves the *they*s wrong with *Not Your Average 5K.* This book will be an invaluable resource for new runners. Jill is like that supportive best friend, chatting with you over coffee, giving you the encouragement and support you need to reach your goals.

The book is a quick, easy read that will have you laughing along the way to preparing for your first race. The best part is, that the program the book provides covers so many aspects that you don't get from any of the couch-to-5K apps including what to wear and how to keep yourself motivated. Plus, *Not Your Average 5K* is not *only for* newbies. After reading Jill's first book, *Running With Curves,* I went from a non-runner to completing several races, including a half-marathon. Even so, I still found plenty of excellent information in *Not Your Average 5K*—some new and some that I'd "forgotten" that I was able to incorporate into my training right away.

So forget what "they" say, read this book, and lace up your running shoes. *Not Your Average 5K* will help you become a runner. In fact, it can help turn anyone into a sparkly, race-running unicorn!

MELISSA CASEY

I love the book. Jill covered EVERYTHING! Looking back on one race I completed, I wish I had seen her race day tips prior. Had I pinned my bib to my shirt the night before, I wouldn't have had to return home to get it. I really like how the acronym tied into the training plan. That was a fun and creative idea. As a seasoned runner, I love that she included assignments and space for writing about your experience. I completed my first half marathon in 2013 and wrote in my journal during the entire training. It's awesome to have something to look back on. This book is great for individual use but would also make a great gift. Running is more fun with friends.

APRIL B.
Creative Director #IRUNTHISC1TY

If you are thinking about participating in a 5k and you aren't sure where to start, this is this book for you. No matter your fitness level, shape, or size, Jill Angie will guide you on your way to train for and complete your first 5k, AND she will do it with knowledge, compassion, experience, and a lot of humor! If you already have a 5k or two under your running shoes, this book is still a great reference. Best of all it comes with a link to training plan that is like getting a whole workbook that will help you bring YOUR goals into focus and give you the tools you need to be the most fabulous you you can be!

MARCY EVICK

This fluffy 50 year old is loving your book! This thorough step-by-step guide is giving me the confidence to try something that I never thought I was capable of. It's lovingly written, straightforward but not preachy. Now to go to Penney's, I think I need a new outfit. Or two.........

JUNE KENNEDY

This book was inspiring and encouraging. As a runner for a few years with a few 5Ks already finished, I wasn't sure how much I would enjoy this book or learn. Jill is funny and encouraging. I struggle with motivation and have a hard time getting out the door and getting my feet moving. *Not Your Average 5K* encouraged me to get off my butt and move. Jill helped me find my motivation. I love the training journal that goes along with this book. It is so great to write down goals, thoughts, and counter-proposals to my excuses. After reading even the first chapter of this book, I went to my computer to start looking up more races. If you have never run and think you can't, you need to read this book. If you find yourself lacking motivation to get out and let your feet hit the pavement, you need to read this book. If you are already running, but need some motivation to sign up for a race, you need to read this book. It is easy to read and will inspire everyone to get out and move. You can do it too!

JESSY NELSON

I have been trying to begin training for a 5K but I just did not know how to start the process. I thought that I could use everything to begin my training in your book! I also liked how detailed your book was and encouraging! I know that I can now start my training for a 5k and be very successful at it!

SANDY MENDES

I absolutely loved this book! It's full of great ideas and tools to help you be the runner that you've always wanted to be. It brought out the strong, fierce, curvaceous runner that I always knew was there but that had been crushed by my inner mean girl! A great read for anyone who wants to fight that Inner Mean Girl (IMG!) but is not sure where to start. Thanks Jill for always being so inspiring and knowing just what to say!

KIM CAMPBELL

If you don't think you fit the mold of what society, or your friends and family, think a runner is, this book is for you! If you've tried other running programs without much progress, this book is for you! If you've never been able to imagine that YOU could be brave enough to sign up for a 5K race, this book is for you! *Not Your Average 5K* is not only a training plan for running a 5K, but also a plan to tackle the obstacle courses of life and training that threaten to get in the way of success.

Jill Angie provides the reader with a friendly and purposeful plan that will definitely deliver results, along with suggestions on clothing, equipment, fuel, motivation, and selecting just the right first 5k race for the best experience. Not Your Average 5K will lift you up, get you going, and get you to the finish line!

DEBBIE IACONIELLO

Not Your Average 5K is a one-stop shop with a wealth of information for new runners. Jill Angie has taken her experiences and concretely set out an easy to follow plan for everyone. What is unique to Jill's book is she starts at the real beginning... Why do you want to do it, and how do you plan to set yourself up for success? Her pre-work alone sets a solid foundation even before the training begins. As an experienced 5K runner, I enjoyed some new tricks and tips. For example, it never would have occurred to me to look at prior year race times to help ensure success when looking for my first race. NYA5K is the first beginner training plan I have read that takes into account not only the physical aspect of running, but the whole experience."

LIZETTE PLOCK

Jill Angie writes with a voice that all women need to hear when they are thinking about running their first 5K. She gives practical running advice in this new book that comes from years of experience and wisdom from working with 100s of women, turning them into 5K success stories. Her warm humor comes through in the book and you will chuckle out loud as she gives you guidelines to make getting to the finish line an enjoyable experience.

I used Jill's first book, *Running with Curves,* back when I became a runner myself. I will now be using this book to train my own clients and will have each of them download the training plan. It's solid and allows each person to define and celebrate their own victories! This is the book to read if you want to take that first step towards discovering or rediscovering the athlete inside you!

AMY DEL GROSSO

Personal trainer, wellness coach and blogger, exclamationpointliving.wordpress.com

I have been overweight (or curvy) for most of my adult life. But for some reason I have always loved running. I have also ran a lot, sometimes only for fun and sometimes races too. Running (and cycling) has felt so natural and easy for me to do, you do not need much stuff to be able to do it. I have also read much about running but always like reading more just for motivation. That's why I practically ate this book in one sitting.

I like the way you present running, that no matter what's your size or backround, you can always run. I started years ago from zero, and love love love running today! I also like that you kept this book short enough to read it at one sitting, or keep reading it again and again to stay motivated. I am sure you will inspire someone (or many) to start running with this book!

KIRSI MALM

(aiming for my 4th half marathon next May)

I have been running now for three years and found some great tips in this book! When I started out, I felt alone and over my head. There was no local group help at the time for new runners, so I joined a running group that met on Tuesdays. Everyone was so far ahead of me; they were the typical fast, thin, fit, people who have been running their whole lives. It was a wonder I didn't quit then and there! If I had this book—I would have known—not all runners look like that or have to run that fast. And, they all knew how to maneuver around the "race experience" which made me feel even more clueless.

While I was reading this book I was thinking, "ok...so there are others like me who have these questions or feelings." Knowing that others felt like beacons out there in their new bright colored, form fitting running clothes—worn for a reason—would have eased the discomfort the first time I walked out the door in them. The section on Race Rules and Logistics; I had no clue about these things when I ran my first race and felt stupid asking them. This book answered those questions and I didn't feel alone anymore because if it made it into this book, that means other newbies have the same questions.

The section that covers the night before your race to after the finish is invaluable to anyone running their first race. I loved how Jill answered questions about races that most participants with experience just assume are common knowledge. I wish I had this book when I started because it breaks it all down to simple, "doable" steps and helps you feel like "if she can do it, so can I and most of all—I'm not alone." Great book! Great tips!

LINDA PITNEY

I wish this book had been available when I started running. Simple and straight forward approach to get off the couch and across the finish line. I love the homework after each lesson! Anyone would be able to achieve their goal with this plan! Not to mention some bragging rights and maybe even bling!! And the cherry on top would be joining this group of badass curvy runners that are truly an inspiration to us all!! Thank you Jill for doing what you do!!

STEPHANIE

There is something so wonderful about being inspired by other women. Let's stop judging each other and instead lift each other up. Jill's book does just that and more. She motivates me to push a little bit more each day and to find a plan that works for me. I love the practical advice and her encouragement. I will be recommending this book to my friends and family.

BRENDA POTTINGER

I completed a half-marathon in May of this past year and then trained all summer for a four miler. I injured myself in the process and have been on the training slump ever since. *Not Your Average 5K: A Practical 8-Week Training Plan for Beginning Runners* is what I have needed to get back into training. Learning from Jill the basics of how to plan and start training for my first 5k (post injury) is exactly what I needed in my life. Setting reasonable expectations, having an easy to follow training plan, and breaking down all the advice you may have been given in the past about what you must have and do to be a "real runner" into the basics of exactly what you need to do is what makes this the perfect training guide for any new or recovering runner. If you're ready to start, start again, or improve, Jill Angie is here for you with her great new book and training plan.

AIMEE C.

This a great book for the beginner and for the runner who may need a quick but thorough reminder of the basics. Each chapter gives you the "how-to's" but what stands out about Jill's book is she carefully explains the "why's" as to get you off on the right foot (pun intended). So many of us just get out there and run. Sure, it's supposed to be that simple, but Jill educates the reader so it CAN be that simple!! Her chapter on Fuel increased my knowledge base on the effects of water on the body and I'm an ultramarathoner!! Jill makes learning to run as easy as walking!

KD RICHARDSON

I've done 9 5Ks and one obstacle course in 2015. I'm far from the slender, fit person you would imagine as a runner. I either walked the entire way or put little sprints in here or there. I wanted something fun to get a head start on weight loss and fitness. I've met some of the most supportive people in my life even when I was dead last across the finish line. This book has motivated me to take the next step by trying the plan and seeing if I can reach the goal of actually running a 5K and beating my previous times! This book is written so well, you can hear the author speak as you are reading. This is truly a quick read packed with valuable information! I'd recommend this to anyone that is trying to become a runner and never thought they could be!

GINA SCHWARTZ

I enjoyed reading the book very much. It I was worded simply and easy to follow. It was like having a series of conversations with the author. I liked the way it flowed and the accompanying workbook was a great addition.

CARLA KRANZ

I have been running on and off for the last four years, and read Jill's first book last year. I always thought I was not really a runner because of being plus size and slower than most people. After having a few different minor injuries and being told I shouldn't run because I am bigger, that it isn't good for me and I would not be successful with it, I was ready to give up on it and put it in my past—until I read this book. After reading this book, Jill has given me the extra push and the will to keep going and to make my dream of running a half marathon one day come true. I will go back to "starting over" with the training plans in this book, which are more user friendly than others I have used. This book has given me the reminder that I can do this and it doesn't matter what anyone says!

MANDY DOTTER

NYA5K is so much more than "practical" how-to advice on how to run. Jill speaks to you as if she was your best friend and biggest cheerleader—anticipating your every need, question, fear and excuse. Funny, knowledgeable, straight forward and supportive how-to advice from a friend who has been in your (running) shoes.

NIKKI KRASSEN

This was like sitting in the living room talking to a friend... such good information in plain English. I love love love the training journal and the pre-training work. I've done many 5Ks, 10Ks, and 6 half marathons. After a few rough health years, I'm trying to get back into running... and this gave me a positive boost and the power to tell IMG to sit down because I've got this. Thank you!!

CHERYL POMERANING

Not Your Average 5K is a wonderful book for beginning and seasoned runners. I love how visualization techniques are used as part of the training logs. The more you "see" it, the more likely you are to believe it and believe in yourself. The book and plan are easy to follow, gives very important information on gear and chafe/blister prevention and most importantly how to defeat your IMG and overcome obstacles. Another great book by Jill Angie!

TERRI MYRE

Jill Angie has done it again! The author of *Running With Curves* has created a helpful tool for all shapes and sizes, experienced and new runners. No matter what walk of running you are, everyone can find something helpful with this book. Many thanks to Jill for the time and effort to help us curvy runners!

RIAN HAHN

I've been a runner for a year now, thanks in large part to Jill Angie's first book, and this second book is just the motivation to breathe life into my running again! This book, with its downloadable training workbook, breaks training for a 5K into doable, small parts so changing your lifestyle and becoming a runner isn't overwhelming. With Ms. Angie's plan, you work through your own personal excuses up front and get them out of your way. As someone that has already run a 5K, I came across a ton of tips that would have made my training and my first race easier... I'll now implement them as I reestablish my running habit.

BRITTNEY YOUNG

This. This is what I had been waiting for. Jill gets it. It's like she was in my head. She understands not only the physical challenges but the mental and emotional challenges of being not your average runner. The plan she has developed is built for success. This is the one that will take you to the finish line. I had started and stopped so many times but Jill's methods, ideas, and strategies made this chronic dropout a runner. This book is the total package. Jill put in everything you need to know to train for and finish that 5K in a realistic way—and answers questions you won't even know to ask :) Thank you for creating the wonderful Not Your Average Runner community, Jill. We needed you.

SUSAN EASON

Whether you've never run a mile in your life or you've finished multiple races, *Not Your Average 5K* offers runners of all paces and abilities the perfect opportunity to begin anew and find their happy pace. Jill Angie offers readers... I mean RUNNERS the perfect mix of valuable information for beginners, new perspective for those who have been around the block once or twice, and authenticity for all.

Even though I've been finding my happy pace since 2011, which has included multiple 5Ks, 10Ks, and nine half marathons, I found myself writing notes in the margins and discovering new ways to tweak my own journey with running. And as a lover of schedules, outlines, lists, and reflection... the training journal that is included is a perfect addition to keep runners responsible and reflective each week, each day, each step along the way. As a fellow "not your average" runner, I highly recommend the read!

HEATHER QUINLAN

This is the book I wished I'd had when I first started running. I've quit C25K so many times because I would get frustrated. *Not Your Average 5K* feels like it was written just for me. Like I had my own personal running coach. I would definitely recommend for any new runners, or for anyone who has been discouraged in the past. I can't wait to see where I am in 2 months!

VALERIE

Just read the book NYA5K and accompanying journal. This is a great primer for a beginner runner as well as someone who has already struggled through a few 5Ks. The program is accessible and gets the runner to examine why they want to run and helps to find the motivation to continue. I am printing out the training journal and going to start the NYA5K program to improve my times. Thanks Jill Angie for creating a program that focuses on more than just the mechanics of running.

APRIL HUGHEY

After trying a couch to 5K program and never finishing in the past, I've become a runner with Jill's help. I ran my first 5K in January and have done a race each month since all the way through training for a 1/2 marathon. Jill knows her stuff and knows the challenges that curvy runners face.

Her new book is even better than her first for new runners in my opinion. It has practical step-by-step directions to teach you all you need to know for your first 5K, or even gather some great tips for those who are already running. It's a quick read for busy people like me and filled with humor too. The book includes training plans, nutrition, stretching, injury prevention, gear recommendations and more.

JESSICA FINDLEY

Jill's latest book made me want to lace up my shoes and run in the rain, motivation and humour together with an easy to follow training plan put my IMG (Inner Mean Girl) in her place once and for all.

LARA EDWARDS

NOT YOUR 5K
AVERAGE

A PRACTICAL 8-WEEK TRAINING PLAN
FOR BEGINNING RUNNERS

by Jill Angie

COPYRIGHT

DISCLAIMER

Cover Design: John Matthews

Interior Design: Heidi Miller

Editing: Kate Makled & Mila Nedeljkov

Author's Photo Courtesy of Jackie Bayne

Cover Photo Courtesy of Andre L. Smith Photography, www.andrelsmith.com

DEDICATION

To my husband Ken, for continuing to believe in my crazy-ass dreams. Thank you for standing by me.

To the *Not Your Average Runner* community. Thank you for being brave and strong and fierce every single day. Without you, there would be no revolution.

To my coach and mentor, Angela Lauria. Thank you for being the person that you are, and for holding the space for so many authors to change the world. I am proud and honored to be a part of the movement.

A LOVE NOTE TO ALL
MY CURVY RUNNING SISTERS

You are just right the way you are. Whatever your last 5K time was...it is amazing. Whatever place you were in your last race, you won.

You look beautiful in that sleeveless running tank, and sexy in those running tights. Your legs are strong and powerful and graceful.

You are not too slow. Not too fat. Not too old.

Your Inner Mean Girl is wrong.

You are gorgeous, amazing and perfect exactly the way you are.

You are a real runner and I am proud of you.

This book is for you.

TABLE OF CONTENTS

INTRODUCTION

Hey there! If you picked up this book, I'm assuming you have a desire, somewhere deep down in your soul, to do a 5K someday—or else you're stuck on a 13 hour flight to Australia with nothing else to do and you found this book stuffed in the seat pocket. Either way, I'm glad you're here! *Not Your Average 5K* is a sequel to my first book, *Running With Curves: Why You're Not Too Fat to Run, and the Skinny on How to Start Today*, but you don't need to have read it to get the most out of this book. Of course, it's a pretty awesome book—both hilarious and educational—so feel free to go get it right now, wink wink.

OK, ready to go? Great! First of all, I have great news for you.

This book is going to rock your world.

Throughout the rest of this book, I'm going to give you everything you need to start and finish your first 5K. You'll get an awesome training program, figure out how to fit running into your packed schedule, learn how to run with proper form and breathing, stay motivated even when you're tired or busy, and fuel your body like a real runner (and I don't mean eating nothing but carrots and protein shakes!). Most importantly, you're going to triumphantly cross that finish line like an absolute rock star.

You're going to get there in just 2 months, too. How are we going to do it? Well, we're going to follow a tried and tested system that I've created called YOUR FIRST 5K. Each letter corresponds to a week in your training program, and has a very specific purpose:

Y do a 5K?

Orient yourself for success

Understand the basics

Resourceful running

Fuel properly

Initiate yourself into the club

Resilient running

Stay motivated when life gets in the way

Try it out—race day rehearsal and strategies for success

5K week, time to put everything together and race!

You'll have a homework assignment for each chapter, as well as three training runs to complete each week. The program is designed to properly build up your strength and endurance so you can show up on race day ready to run and have a blast.

If you're thinking "But I've already done a 5K, this isn't the book for me," I have good news. You can still get a lot out of this book! It's not just for brand-new beginners, and even if you've got a few under your belt already, I guarantee you'll learn something new.

Before we jump in, however, I need you to do a few things. First, make sure you read the entire book before you officially start the training plan. I know you're excited to get started, but I promise that taking a few hours to read everything from start to finish will give you the best chance of success. It's short. Draw a scented bubble bath, pour a glass of wine, and carve out the next couple of hours just for you. Or hide out in your car with a latte while the kids are at soccer practice. It's all good. You're officially on your way to your first 5K and that's all that matters.

After you're done reading, download and print your training plan at www.notyouraveragerunner.com/5k-book. This will be your guide for everything you do throughout the rest of this book[1].

Finally—and this might be the most important step of all—pick out a reward for yourself for hitting your goal! It can be anything at all—as simple as treating yourself to a celebratory meal with your family, or a super deluxe payoff like getting a new kitchen (like one of my clients did, and she still hasn't invited me over for dinner!). Whatever you choose, make sure it is meaningful to you, because you'll use it to help boost your motivation throughout the process. Write it down on a post-it note and stick it on your fridge. And here's an idea: take a picture of your note and email it to me at reward@NotYourAverageRunner.com—and I'll check back with you in two months to see if you've earned it yet!

---

1 You might be wondering why I didn't just include the plan at the back of the book, and there are a few reasons for that. First, this is a small book, and the plan is on letter-sized paper—which gives you a lot more space to write. Second, if you wanted to go through the program again, you can print the plan all over again and have a clean place to record your progress. And finally, because it will allow me to keep in touch with you if I add anything to the plan in the future!

Who is this book for?

This book is for anyone (and I mean AN-Y-ONE) who wants to complete their first 5K. That means you don't even have to be a runner right now. As long as you can walk for 3 miles, you will be able to do a 5K in two months. I promise. Also, this book is designed to train you to finish that 5K in a way that feels good to you, both mentally and physically. That means you can walk, run, skip, or even disco dance your way across the finish line. Now, if you've already done a 5K (or two... or five), this doesn't mean you won't get anything out of this book. Just the opposite, in fact. There is a truckload of helpful information here that will help you take your 5K performance to the next level.

Not convinced yet? OK, fine. Let me introduce you to a couple of my favorite people.

Meet Cindy.

Cindy just turned 46, has a 9-year old son, and weighs about 75 pounds more than she'd like to. She's stopped and started a ton of fitness programs in the past—always with the best of intentions—but each and every time she loses interest after a couple of weeks and now her bedroom closet has a shameful pile of yoga mats, kettle bells and fitness bands gathering dust. Every time her husband complains about it, she's all, "Oh, I'm going to start using those next week!" but another month comes and goes and soon there's another fitness gadget added to the pile.

She knows her husband loves her and supports her, but she's totally lost her sexy spark and feels old and frumpy. She used to love to get dressed up to go out, but lately she'd rather stay on the couch with her family and a big pile of take-out food. She's too damn tired all the time to do anything else.

Still, she does go for a walk around the neighborhood a few times a month, and even throws in an occasional jogging interval when she thinks nobody is looking. In fact, one time she ran for a minute straight and felt like such a badass. That night, she dreamed about running effortlessly like a Kenyan. It was amazing.

The next morning she woke up and told her husband and he laughed his ass off.

"You? Running? Um, I hate to break it to you honey, but your track record for exercise is pretty bad. You're just not the type of person that likes to move."

Grrrr. Sometimes she thinks that doing a 5K would be the best revenge, if for no other reason than to prove other people wrong.

Then her son chipped in:

"Yeah Mom, the last time we went on vacation you just sat and read a book while everyone else went for a bike ride. But that's OK, if you got all skinny I wouldn't be able to use your tummy as a pillow when we're watching TV."

Ooof. That one really hurt.

The truth is, Cindy does enjoy her occasional walks and believes she could do a 5K or even a longer distance. Her problem is that she stalls out every time she thinks about all that's involved. Making time in her busy schedule. Finding cute running clothes that fit and don't make her look like an elephant. Learning how to breathe properly. Getting the courage to actually sign up for a race. It's flat-out overwhelming and keeps her on the couch.

But she knows that if she sets a goal and goes public with it, she's less likely to back out. After giving it some thought, Cindy picks a small, local 5K about 2 months away and signs up. She marks it on her calendar and (gulp) tells her family. They laugh and say they'll believe it when they see it.

"Game on!" Cindy thinks.

Cindy's challenges will be reprogramming her established habits by creating new ones. She will also have to manage her beliefs that her husband and son see her as a quitter. The good news is that once Cindy begins to see herself as someone who follows through on her commitments, her family will be able to view her that way too. She will need to remember that running will feel hard at first, but that doesn't mean she's not good at it—the longer she sticks with it, the easier it will get.

Now meet Sarah.

Sarah is 37, with two daughters aged ten and four. She's got an amazing career and gets promoted year after year, and always gets complimented on how competent and confident she is at work. And she's making a ton of money, which means her family can have a gorgeous home and take some really fabulous vacations. From the outside, she has a dream life.

But inside, she feels like a total failure. She's struggled with body image for most of her life, and despite losing 124 pounds three years ago (and hitting her goal weight in just 18 months!) she still hates what she sees when she looks in the mirror. This is a huge disappointment because Sarah really believed that losing weight would make everything perfect.

To top it all off, she has to stay pretty active to maintain her weight loss. Spin class on Saturday mornings, elliptical and a few weight machines before work on Tuesdays and Thursdays, and most nights she walks for 30 minutes on the treadmill in her bedroom, which is when she catches up on her Netflix queue. She's getting pretty good at it too—she can knock out a little over two miles during that time.

Her sister keeps telling her she should start running, but *seriously*?! Sure, she works out a lot, but she's no athlete. Sarah's butt still wobbles and she will never get rid of all that loose skin on her belly and arms without surgery. Wearing a skimpy little tank top—or worse, just a sports bra (which is what runners wear, right?)—is out of the question. Runners are teeny tiny women with perfect bodies and flat stomachs. There's no way in hell she'll ever be a runner. She just doesn't fit in.

Then one day her 9-year old asked to sign up for Girls on the Run during the next school year.

Crap.

This would be an awesome program for her daughter to join, because it not only teaches girls how to run, it also gives them life skills and confidence and teaches them to feel good about themselves.

But if her girls start running, won't they need a training partner? And shouldn't that be her?

Suddenly, Sarah is motivated to at least give it a try, because this is a great opportunity to spend time with her daughter and talk about body image and self-confidence. She's a little worried about keeping up, but she'll do anything to make her kids happy. So she gets her oldest registered for the program the next day, and shifts her schedule around so she can run while her daughter is at practice twice a week. Afterwards, they will chat about their progress in the car on the way home.

Like Cindy, Sarah will also have to manage her beliefs about herself. Despite being successful at weight loss and already a regular exerciser, Sarah does not see herself as an athlete because—in her opinion—she doesn't look like one. To get past this, Sarah will need to believe that athletes come in all shapes and sizes and that the appearance of her body has nothing to do with her fitness level. This will have a huge impact on her daughters too—because when they see their mom feeling confident, they'll naturally follow along.

Both Cindy and Sarah are very typical stories of someone who is not your average runner: someone who wasn't a "skinny mini" in high school, and for whom physical activity does not come easily. The good news is both of these amazing women went on to train for and complete their first 5K, had a ton of fun doing it, and even continued running afterwards. And you can too!

If you're still not quite sure, let me tell you a little about myself.

I'm 48, and I've been a runner, off and on, since 1998. During that time, my weight has fluctuated between 180 and 280 pounds—more than once—but it has never impacted my ability to train for and complete dozens of races, from 5K's to half marathons to triathlons.

When I first started running, a 5K wasn't even on my radar. I just wanted to lose weight, and decided to run laps around my block. Since I couldn't go more than 30 seconds at a time, that's exactly where I started. I would sprint for 30 seconds, completely out of breath, and walk for a minute or two to recover, over and over again until I'd completed four laps (two miles). Back then, most people didn't know about the run/walk interval method, they just kept adding a few minutes to their workout until they were running the entire time (or they gave up, because that's a *really* hard way to train for a 5K). As you'd expect, I got plenty of raised eyebrows and funny looks from my neighbors, all of them wondering why I was running like I was being chased by a bear and then suddenly stopping to walk.

This was in the middle of one of the hottest summers on record in eastern PA, and almost every run was difficult and uncomfortable. Most of the time, I thought I was going to pass out from the heat. At the time, cute workout clothes never came in anything larger than a size L, so I ran in long, thick cotton leggings, stretched so tightly I was always waiting for them to rip, and covered up the rest of my body in enormous men's cotton t-shirts that hung to my knees.

Needless to say, I sweated my ass off that summer, but eventually I got stronger, running a couple of minutes at a time, and learned how to pace myself so that I was jogging at a comfortable pace instead of racing around like a lunatic. It even started to feel good, and I began to realize that my life in general felt so much easier when I ran regularly.

Then someone told me about a local 5K. I had no idea such a thing existed, but it sounded like fun so I signed up and started training in earnest.

Race day came, and I lined up to start with 100 others who looked like real athletes—thin, fit, and wearing actual running clothes. I felt totally out of place. When the starting gun went off, I quickly found myself at the back of the pack.

There was a choice to be made: I could feel bad about being left in the dust and suffer for the entire event, or I could run at my own speed without stressing out, giving it my best effort while having fun. I chose the latter, and finished in 42 minutes. Because there were only 100 runners, I was almost dead last. But it was one of the proudest moments of my life because that was the moment I knew I was a runner.

It was so powerful that years later I still get teary thinking about how it felt to cross that finish line. I want you to have that feeling too.

Y: WHY DO A 5K?

You will have the best chance of success if you begin by getting mentally ready to start the training process. Knowing exactly why you want to take on this challenge, and preparing ammunition for those moments when your motivation disappears, will help you stick with it during the difficult moments (and there will be a few, I promise).

It's all about your attitude, really. Once you get your head in the right space, the rest of this will be ridiculously easy—you'll literally just put one foot in front of the other until you're done.

We'll focus on that prep work in this chapter, and also work on setting up your schedule for success and making sure you have the basic gear. Then it's time to start running.

This includes six steps, and it shouldn't take you more than an hour:

1. Know WHY you want to do a 5K

2. Anticipate what your objections/excuses might be

3. Formulate counter-proposals to those thoughts

4. Imagine what you'll be like in two months after you've finished your 5K

5. Get your equipment ready

6. Reserve the time

STEP 1: Know your "why."

Everyone's WHY is personal, but I've found that there are a few common reasons many people can relate to. Try some of these on for size:

I want to...

- motivate myself to get regular exercise

- keep up with my kids

- have something really cool that I can be proud of doing

- prove to my spouse that I'm not a quitter

- prove to *myself* that I'm not a quitter

- feel better in my clothes

- get a little extra help losing weight

- take time out for myself spend time with friends

- get a free banana and t-shirt

- raise money for my favorite charity

- finally have something to brag about at work on Monday mornings

- get my diabetes under control

- have an excuse to go shopping for new workout clothes

Can you see yourself anywhere in that list?

Finding your own "why" is one of the most important pieces of this journey, because without it you'll lose interest pretty quickly.

Both Cindy and Sarah found their "why" before they started training. Cindy wanted to prove to her family that she wasn't a quitter, and maybe even lose a little weight. Sarah realized that running could be something really important to share with her daughter, and it would give them an opening to talk about self-esteem, self-care, and setting goals.

STEP 1 ASSIGNMENT:

Take some time to think about all the reasons you want to do a 5K, and write them down in the prep section of your training plan. If you haven't downloaded and printed it yet, make sure you do that first. You can get it at www.notyouraveragerunner.com/5k-book.

Done? Good. Keep that list handy, because you'll be looking at it frequently.

STEP 2:
Anticipate your objections and excuses.

If you think this step doesn't apply to you, you're wrong. It's human nature to resist change and effort. Running is both. Just humor me, and spend a few minutes brainstorming all the possible reasons you might have for failing—from things that could go wrong on race day to excuses you might come up with for skipping a workout. I know you have some hanging out in the back of your mind, because if you didn't you would have already finished a 5K and you wouldn't have bought this book!

Some common objections:

- No motivation
- Hard time breathing when running
- Negative self talk (too slow, too fat, too out of shape)
- Concerned about getting injured
- I can't take time away from my family, they need me too much
- Worried about coming in last or not finishing
- Not knowing how to train properly
- Feeling out of place among so many "real" runners
- No confidence that you can do it
- Don't have time
- Can't get up in the morning
- Might have to take walk breaks

Do any of these sound familiar? If you've already started running, you may have conquered a few, or even most of this list. Woohoo! If not, don't worry, we're going to work on it together.

STEP 2 ASSIGNMENT:

In your training journal, write down all the reasons and excuses you can think of that might prevent you from following through on your commitment.

STEP 3:
Formulate your counter-proposals.

Now it's time to fight back. For each objection, think about how you will create a response that gets you what you want.

For example:

Objection: I can't take time away from my family, they need me too much.

Counter-proposal: My family does need me, but they need me at my best. Taking 45 minutes, three times a week, to follow my training plan means I am taking care of myself so that I can be the best possible version of me.

Objection: I might come in last.

Counter-proposal: That's not the end of the world. First place and last place both have to go the same distance. I will finish, and I'm going to be really proud of that no matter what.

Objection: I hate getting up early in the morning but I don't have time after work.

Counter-proposal: I will only do this twice a week, and save one training run for the weekend. The toughest part about running first thing in the morning is getting out of bed, which only takes 5 seconds. Once I'm up and moving, it's actually not that hard to start my workout.

It's important to be really honest with yourself during this step, because you and your Inner Mean Girl are probably going to have a few heart-to-heart talks during the next few months. She's going to throw up roadblocks and you'll have to knock them down. If you're not prepared with a response, she might get the best of you. (Your Inner Mean Girl is kind of like your negative alter-ego. She's that voice that whispers in your ear: You are too fat to finish a 5K. She's wrong. You can learn more about her, and how to keep her in check, in my first book, *Running With Curves: Why You're Not Too Fat to Run, and the Skinny on How to Start Today*.)

Sometimes there will be legitimate reasons for missing or rescheduling a workout. Life happens, kids fall out of trees and break their arms, or traffic jams cause you to be late. Make sure you have a backup plan in your toolkit for how you'll get past it (we'll talk more about that shortly).

STEP 3 ASSIGNMENT:

For each objection, write down your counter-proposals— the things you'll tell yourself when those objections pop up.

STEP 4:
Tell your coffee shop story.

You know when someone says, "What would you do if you won a million dollars?" Suddenly you are probably imagining how awesome life would be, all the cool stuff you could do, all the amazing things you'd accomplish.

Well, Step 4 is kinda like that. You're going to harness the fun of visualizing your success to make sure you cross that finish line. I call it your "coffee shop story," the story you're going to tell when you run into a friend at your local coffee shop, and they say:

"Wow, I really admire you! I've never thought that a 5K was something I could do. Can you tell me how you did it?"

Then, you'll proudly tell them exactly how you got from just an idea to finish line. What it felt like to go through the training process, how you overcame obstacles that came up along the way, the things you did to make it happen every week even when you were tired and busy, and most importantly what you did on race day—from getting up early and eating your pre-race breakfast, to lining up at the start, through miles one, two and three—and finally what it felt like to cross that finish line.

The thing is, you're going to write this story before you even take a single step in your training. Imagining exactly how you got from here to there, in detail, allows your brain to go to work on making it happen. It sounds woo-woo. I get it. But it also works.

When you're telling your story, include as many details as possible to help you with the visualization. Start by filling in the following sentence and go from there:

It wasn't always easy, but I did it because ____(fill in your WHY)____, even though ____(fill in one or two of your objections)_____. I planned and stuck with it by telling myself _____(fill in your counter-proposals)_____ and it was totally worth it!

STEP 4 ASSIGNMENT:

Write your Coffee Shop Story in your training plan and practice telling it to friends and family!

STEP 5:
Get your equipment ready.

Running is a pretty simple sport, all you need is a trail, a sidewalk, or an open treadmill and you're ready to roll. However, there are lots of ways to enhance your experience and show off your personal style. Navigating the world of running shoes, clothing, and gadgets can be daunting, so in week 5 (**I**nitiate yourself into the club) we'll talk about it in detail. For right now, however, this list presents the minimum you need to get going:

Shoes

For the next few weeks, it's OK to run in whatever athletic shoes you have as long as they are in good shape. They don't need to be running shoes, but make sure they have some cushioning and are meant for exercise. Shoes that you've been wearing everywhere for the last two years, the ones that are all beat up and worn out, aren't the best choice for running. Toss them out or keep them for yard work.

Running clothes

Whatever you have at the moment is fine. Synthetic materials are better than cotton, but, right now, getting you up and running is more important than having the perfect gear.

Tops should be somewhat fitted—not super tight, but also not baggy. Workout tights (or leggings, depending on where you live), either long or short, are a great choice for running. Loose shorts tend to ride up between your thighs, which means you spend a lot of time trying to tug them back into place instead of concentrating on your run. Also, the seams will chafe, and chafing sucks. If you don't have tights right now, head over to Walmart, Target or Old Navy and pick up an inexpensive pair to get you started.

Keeping your hair and sweat out of your eyes is important! Find a hat, headband or visor that will stay in place while you're running. Hats and visors are great if it's sunny, and also if it's raining during a run, because they will keep the rain out of your eyes. If you don't have one, you can pick one up at Walmart or Target for a few dollars.

Timer

You'll need something to time your run/walk intervals. It can be as simple as a smartphone app or an inexpensive clip-on digital timer.

If you like running with your phone, there are dozens of free apps that will keep track of when it's time to run and walk, and even call them out for you. RunKeeper and MapMyRun are two of my favorites.

If you prefer not to use your phone, I suggest ordering a Gymboss timer for ~ $20 on Amazon. This is one of my favorites because it is rugged and easy to use. It has a beep or vibrate option to notify you when the interval is over.

STEP 5 ASSIGNMENT:

Go through your closet and assess what gear you currently have that will work, and then create a shopping list of anything else you need. Use the guide in your training plan.

STEP 6:
Reserve the time.

If you fail to plan, you plan to fail. I know you've heard that statement before, and it couldn't be truer for running. There may be a few lucky women out there who don't have jam-packed schedules, but I know you're not one of them. Which means you'll need to do a realistic assessment of your schedule, and figure out when you're going to get your three runs in each week. Plan to block out 45 minutes to an hour for each one.

Morning exercisers tend to be more consistent, for the simple reason that getting it done before your day gets crazy means your workout isn't something that falls by the wayside later on. That being said, plenty of people are able to make evenings work for them—so if that's when you have time, that's totally fine!

Whichever you choose, make sure to remove as many barriers and excuses as possible ahead of time.

For morning runners:

- Lay out your clothes the night before (or pack your gym bag and *put it in the car*).

- Place your alarm clock on the other side of the room so you actually have to get out of bed to turn it off.

- Shift some of your morning activities to the night before to give yourself more time.

- Go to bed a little earlier to make sure you're well-rested.

- Train your spouse to push you out of bed when the alarm goes off.

- If you have a running buddy, make a date so you know someone will be waiting for you—this works particularly well if said running buddy has no issues with publicly shaming you for not showing up.

- Make sure your phone, GPS watch or other devices are fully charged (or charging) before you go to bed.

- Keep your training plan and your objections/counter-proposals on your phone or in your nightstand, and review them if you want to sleep in.

- When the alarm goes off, tell yourself all you need to do is put on your workout clothes and shoes. Once that's done, tackle the next step.

For evening runners:

- If you are planning to stop at your gym or a trail on the way home from work, pack your bag the night before and *put it in the car*.

- Keep a spare set of everything (clothes, sports bra, ponytail holder, sneakers, socks, even headphones) in your car and bag.

- Run at work, if possible, or choose a gym or trail that are on your way home.

- If you run in your neighborhood, get dressed to run at work—when you get home, don't even go in the house, just hop out of the car and start running.

- Make sure you have a small pre-run snack available to eat in the afternoon.

- Listen to energizing music in the car on the way home from work to get yourself pumped up.

- Plan to meet a buddy for your run.

If you have a flexible work schedule, try running at lunch or another time during the day. And, if you're an at-home mom with little ones to take care of, running strollers have come a long way. Taking your child with you on your workout makes her happy too!

STEP 6 ASSIGNMENT:

Plan out at least your first 2 weeks' worth of runs by reviewing the above guidelines and then entering them into your calendar. Generate a reminder on your phone too; until you create the habit, it's easy to forget!

OK. that's about it for prep work. Print out your training plan and complete steps 1–6 above. It shouldn't take more than an hour—and then you are officially cleared for takeoff—it's time to run!

PUT IT INTO PRACTICE

Cindy's biggest challenges were reprogramming herself for new habits, and seeing herself as someone who keeps her exercise commitments. Writing and practicing her Coffee Shop Story was a key part of her success, because it helped her imagine not just finishing her race, but also how she got there. Here's what she wrote before starting the program:

"It wasn't easy—two months of following a training plan even on those days when all I wanted to do was flop on the couch after work and order pizza. In the beginning, I struggled with that a lot. But, I kept reminding myself that I wanted to prove to myself and my family that I could stick with it, and quitting was not an option. Some days it was all I could do just to get out the door for 10 minutes, but after a couple of weeks, I began to feel so much better about myself that it was easier and easier to choose running instead of watching TV, and when I was three weeks into the program my husband actually brought me flowers one day and said he was impressed with how hard I was working!

There were days when I felt old or embarrassed to run in public in my new running clothes (even though I secretly loved wearing them because they are really colorful)... but there were also days when I felt like a deer leaping across a meadow! It amazed me how good running could feel, and how it got easier over time.

On race day morning, I was so nervous but I kept telling myself that I'd already practiced running the distance, so the race was just another workout with a lot of people cheering me on. I could barely eat my pre-race banana and peanut butter, so I only had half. It was so exciting to be around so many other runners at once and I was surprised to see all shapes, sizes and ages of people there, and I actually ran into another woman from work who was about my size and age. We decided to line up together at the start and talked about how both of us were doing our first race.

When the gun went off, we stuck together until the pack thinned out a bit, then we each followed our own pace and interval plan. After I started running, my whole body relaxed and I fell into my training rhythm for the rest of the race. It was actually really fun—spectators with funny signs and lots of people cheering us on. I went into a full-out run about a quarter-mile before the finish line and crossed it with my hands waving in the air!

All in all, it was totally worth it and seeing the look on my son's face when he saw me cross the finish line was a moment I will never forget."

0: ORIENT YOURSELF FOR SUCCESS
WEEK 1 OF TRAINING

Are you ready? It's time to run! The next 9 chapters will take your through your entire training program from week 1 through race day. Running is so much more than just putting one foot in front of the other, so each chapter will focus on a critical topic on your path to 5K.

This week's lesson will lay foundation for the next two months, including your mindset, picking a goal race that aligns with your skills and expectations, and understanding the basics of run/walk intervals.

Mindset

I promise that the next couple of months will be fun, but also challenging. You will need to remain focused and calm, effectively deal with any obstacles that arise, while also maintaining excitement about reaching your 5K goal.

It all starts with setting expectations.

When you sign up for a 5K, everyone will want to know how fast you run. After you've crossed the finish line, every-one will want to know your finish time. These are the standard, (and annoying) conversations that all non-runners want to have with runners (right up there with "how far was your marathon?").

Now, you probably do know someone who has run a 5K in under 30 minutes, maybe even under 20. The elites can run them in under 15, covering three miles in less than 5 minutes each. That is crazy fast; it means running over 12 mph, which is faster than most people ride their bikes.

Elite runners have been training their entire lives to run fast. They say no to cupcakes, wine, and pizza year-round, in order to carve every last gram of extra fat off their bodies. They are built for speed, and probably have been running competitively since they were twelve years old. Most of them have legs about as big around as my bicep. They are the cheetahs of the human race, and we will marvel at their grace and speed, but be under no illusions that normal people run that fast.

Since you are new to 5K training, chances are very good that it will take you more than 30 minutes. In fact, I suggest planning on finishing at around 45–50 minutes.

This is just an estimate, and some of you will be faster, some slower. Your pace does not make you any more or less of a runner, it's just a number. You will also get faster the next time. But that is irrelevant. If you take anything else away from this chapter, remember this:

Your finish time is not important.

The goal of this race is to train properly and safely, give it your best effort, and most importantly, to have fun. Showing up at the starting line *is* the accomplishment. Everything else is just icing on the cupcake.

Now, I know there are a few of you—and you know who you are—who will still set a time goal for themselves and try to beat it. I get it, and that's totally fine. If you're a competitive person by nature, the very idea of running a race without trying to win (or at least place) is confusing, if not frustrating. If competition is what drives you and keeps you motivated, then—by all means—give yourself a goal to shoot for.

But please, as a personal favor to me, do not use it as a tool to beat yourself up. If you don't make your goal time, you are not a failure. It's a data point, a representation of all the factors of race day—including many that are outside of your control.

Today, you are a beginner. Each week you will get faster and stronger, and it will happen quicker than you think. This is one of the joys of being new to running: endurance builds up quickly, and you begin to expect that each coming week will be easier than the last.

Eventually, you will reach a plateau, where you don't improve as quickly as before. This could happen in a few weeks, or perhaps a few months. There is absolutely no reason to freak out when it happens. The performance plateau is completely normal and happens to everyone. It means you've been training long enough to move beyond the brand-new beginner stage. This is actually cause for celebration!

You will have days when running feels harder than normal, and days when it feels easy. This is normal as well, and it happens to everyone. It does not mean you are a bad runner or a failure. It means you are human.

There will be days when you just don't feel like running. You're tired, or it's raining, or you'd rather go out to happy hour with your friends. Unless you are injured, run anyway. For at least 10 minutes. After that, you have my permission to quit. Maintaining the habit of exercise, even if it is for 10 minutes, is crucial. Skipping a few workouts won't ruin your physical fitness, but it will begin to erode your habit. A new habit is hard to form, so don't waste what you've already built. If you have a training run on your schedule, do it for 10 minutes, so you can keep your momentum going.

There will be days when everything goes wrong—and your carefully planned schedule goes out the window. You will be tempted to give up your run to make time for other things, but I urge you to look carefully at your day and see if there is something else you can skip. As I mentioned above, missing one workout will not cause you to lose any training ground (in fact, sometimes an unexpected rest day can make your next run really amazing). The problem with skipping a run because you're busy is that when you find out that there is little to no impact on your training, it becomes easy to justify missing the next one. Allowing yourself to renege on your commitment for any reason other than injury or a true emergency can be the start of a very a slippery slope—and next thing you know, two weeks have gone by, and now you're in trouble.

If you start thinking about your run as the most important thing you'll do that day, it becomes easier to find a way to fit it in.

So promise me this. On those days when you think you're too busy, or you just don't feel like it, go anyway. For at least 10 minutes. After that, you can quit. This will maintain the habit, as well as your endurance (and of course once you get to the end of 10 minutes you'll probably finish your workout).

Did I mention just do it for 10 minutes?

Choosing the Perfect First Race

The race you choose to do can have an impact on your performance, both physically and mentally. So, before you sign up and hand over your credit card information to the race organizer, make sure the event meets your needs.

Location

Convenience is one of the most important factors. The closer it is to home, the easier it will be to get to the starting line on race day (eliminating a potential source of stress), and you might even be able to do a practice run of the course during your training. At the very least, you'll be able to drive it and get familiar with landmarks and where the hills are. Aim to find one within a 45-minute drive of your home, so you don't have to get up at the butt-crack of dawn, or stay overnight in an unfamiliar bed.

The exception to this rule is when you're already going to be traveling to the area for other reasons such as vacation or visiting family. In this case, if you have enough time to prepare, doing a race near where you're staying can be a great way to enhance your trip.

Time limits

Look for a race that is "walker friendly," which usually indicates there is no time limit (or if there is, it is a generous one). It also means that the race organizers expect many people to take an hour or so to finish, and there will still be race support at the finish line and lots of people to cheer you on. Alternatively, if you find an event that takes place at the same time as longer distance races (for example there is a 5K, 10K and a half marathon), chances are excellent that this will be a race that is appropriate for beginners as well, because the race organizer will be keeping the finish line open for a few hours.

Untimed theme races, such as Color Runs, are great. They're usually lots of fun, and have an awesome party for finishers. However, if you're looking for more of a true race experience, these might not be the best choice, because there will likely be large groups of people on the course walking at a slow pace. If you think you'll get frustrated if there are people in your way (especially if you're hoping to run a certain time), this is not the best first 5K for you.

Check finishing times from previous years (usually available on the race website). If you think you'll finish in about 45 minutes, make sure that at least one person from the prior year finished at that time. If this is a race where most people are done in 30 minutes, you will potentially be setting yourself up for an awkward situation.

Terrain

If you train on a hilly course, you're pretty much prepared for anything. But if most of your training will be done on flat roads, or on a treadmill, you don't want to pick a course with rolling hills for your first. Also: a trail run 5K, even if it is flat as a pancake, requires different skills than one that takes place on pavement.

To find out more about the race you're considering, read all the information on the race website. If there isn't one, or if the information you are looking for isn't there (as is sometimes the case with small races), email or call the race director.

If possible, ask people who have done that race in the past. In particular, people who are not experienced runners, or are traditionally running at the "back of the pack," as they will be able to give you an honest opinion (rather than someone who routinely does sub-30 5Ks).

If all else fails, check to see if the race has a Facebook page, or if anyone at your local running store has done it in the past.

Run/walk intervals— and your first week's training plan

Throughout the next 2 months, you'll be doing three training runs per week. There are two plans, named after two of my favorite people: Cindy and Sarah.

Follow the *Cindy* plan if you're brand new to running, especially if you've never run before.

Follow the *Sarah* plan if you've been working out regularly for at least 6 months and/or have been experimenting with running for a few months.

If you're not sure which applies to you, choose the Cindy plan. As you gain experience with running, you can switch. Conversely, if you find that the Sarah plan is too challenging, you can drop back to Cindy. It's all good.

Each plan is based on a progression of run/walk intervals, increasing the amount of running and decreasing the total amount of walking over time. However, neither plan requires you to run the entire 5K at the end, although you might find you are able to.

Why run/walk intervals?

Well, to start with, most people can't just pick up and run 3.1 miles without training. You could probably run for 5 minutes or so if you had to, but after that there's a chance you'd be so completely out of breath (with a side stitch to boot), that you'd have to stop, lean over, and puke.

Well-defined run/walk intervals, where you run for a short period of time and then actively recover with a brisk walk, will help you build up your cardiorespiratory and muscular endurance without risking injury (or causing your breakfast to end up on the sidewalk).

Over time, you will be able to run farther and faster in between walk breaks. You will also complete your distance faster overall, despite walking. It's counter-intuitive, but it works. Walk breaks make faster runners.

To get the most out of your intervals, your timer will be the boss of you. When it beeps to run, you run. When it beeps to walk, you walk (even if you still feel like running). It's important to take your walk breaks *before* your legs are tired, because this will allow them to recover quickly and be ready for the next running period. It will ensure that you can go farther and finish faster overall, and feel great the next day.

The other important reason to use a timer is that it takes the responsibility for keeping track of your intervals off your shoulders. I know it would be easy to just use a digital watch or count in your head, but trust me...that will be a huge distraction. And while you're watching the clock for the end of your run you'll trip on a curb and skin your knee. I know, because I've done it. Allow the timer to do the work for you and you'll have a much better experience.

Pacing

Remember that the run part of run/walk is not a sprint. You are not being chased by a bear. Think comfortable jogging pace: faster than a walk, but not so fast that in 30 seconds you will be gasping for air.

Conversely, the walk portion is not a stroll. You are not shopping at the mall. When the timer goes off, 3–5 seconds of slow walking is all you need. Then it's time to pick up the pace and walk briskly until the timer signals time to run again.

Before every workout, you must warm up with 5 minutes of walking. Yes, it's boring. I get it. You don't want to waste precious workout time with warming up; you want to get to the fun part! But that 5-minute walk is actually part of your workout, and it is non-negotiable. Warming up gets your heart, lungs and muscles ready to run.

Don't believe me? Try to do your entire workout without a warmup, and see how fast you end up with a side stitch, shin splints, and gasping for air.

Or you could just take my word for it.

After your workout is complete, walk for another 3–5 minutes to allow your heart, lungs and muscles to return to normal. While you're running, your arteries expand to accommodate the extra circulation to your muscles. It takes a little while for them to go back to normal, and slow walking after your run is complete is important in order to allow for this to happen gradually. If you just stop and sit down, you'll end up feeling dizzy and lightheaded.

WEEK 1 HOMEWORK

Look over your Week 1 training plan, and familiarize yourself with the intervals. Program your timer, phone app, or running watch ahead of time so you don't have to fiddle around with it mid-run. Make sure you can hear the prompts or feel the buzzer.

If you're not running on a treadmill, plan your route ahead of time so you don't have any last minute confusion about where to go. Leave yourself enough time for a 5-minute warmup walk, as well as a 5-minute cool-down walk. Check the weather, and tell someone where you'll be when you're running, in case of emergency.

After each run, take a few moments to make some quick notes in your training plan. Follow the prompts (date, time, weather, etc.) or record whatever is important to you.

It's time to go!

PUT IT INTO PRACTICE

Sarah chose to run twice a week while her daughter was at her Girls on the Run practice. At the first meeting, she found herself watching the coaches and comparing her body to theirs, and falling short. But, she remembered her main objection (I'm not built like a runner, my butt jiggles and I'm not an athlete) and her counter-proposal (Everyone has to start somewhere, and nobody else cares what my butt looks like. I'm setting a good example for my daughter and helping her become a confident young woman) and went on her first-ever run.

She struggled a little in the beginning with figuring out how fast to run, but eventually it started to feel more natural and she even found herself enjoying the rhythm of the intervals. When her workout was over she was even a little disappointed because she wanted to do more!

U: UNDERSTAND THE BASICS
WEEK 2 OF TRAINING

You did it! You finished your first week of 5K training! You are officially a rock star now.

Week 1 was all about getting in the right mindset and practicing what it's like to run intervals with a timer. This week, we're going to get a little more technical and talk about breathing, listening to your body and proper running form.

Breathing

The number one complaint I hear from new runners is this:

"I get completely out of breath when I run."

The smarty-pants inside me wants to answer, "Um yeah, running is cardio, of course you're going to be breathing hard."

But what they really mean when they say they can't breathe is that they're so out of breath they can't continue. And that's a problem we can do something about!

The faster you run, the harder you work. The harder you work, the more oxygen your muscles need. Since the only way to get more oxygen to the muscles is to inhale more, you start to breathe faster. At some point, your lungs reach a point where they are completely maxed out, and you can't go any faster.

Over time, your body will become more efficient as you adapt to the stress of running, and you will be able to go faster and farther. However, there will always be a point where your lungs just can't keep up.

The good news is, there are lots of ways to keep yourself running without getting to that point. It starts with evaluating your effort level.

The Borg 10-point *Rate of Perceived Exertion* (RPE) scale will help you understand if you're running too fast for your body's capabilities.

Here's how it works:

The scale runs from 0-10, with 0 being at complete rest, and 10 being maximum effort (such as being chased by a mountain lion).

0—Nothing at all

1—Very light

2—Fairly light

3—Moderate

4—Somewhat hard

5—Hard

6

7—Very hard

8

9

10—Very, very hard

At a 0, you're lying on the couch, binge-watching Netflix.

At a 1–2, you're window shopping at the mall, and at 3, you're hustling to Old Navy so you can score a deal on workout gear before they sell out of your size. This is also your warmup pace: brisk walking, with purpose.

From 4–6, you're in the run/walk zone. Your heart is beating faster, your breathing is deeper and more rapid. You're putting in some effort. At a 4–5, you could probably keep up this pace for 20 minutes if you had to, at a 6, maybe 10 minutes. The endorphins will start to flow at this pace, and you might even feel the mythical runner's high.

A 7–8 is a pretty big effort, and you could keep it up for a couple of minutes but that's about it. Think running to catch a bus, or dashing through the rain to get in the house.

At 9 or 10, you're in an all-out sprint as if your life depended on it. You probably couldn't keep this pace up for more than 30 seconds.

Here's how all of the above applies to your training:

During your warmup walk, get yourself to an RPE of 3—walking with purpose, but comfortably. You're preparing your body to run.

For the run/walk interval portion of your workout, aim to stay in the range of 4–6. This will keep you breathing at an elevated but still comfortable rate, maintainable for your entire workout.

When you're running, aim for a 5; when you're walking, a 3–4.

During your cool-down walk, bring it back to a 3, then a 2. You heart rate and breathing will slowly come back to normal.

Note that none of the above criteria are tied to a specific pace per mile! Everyone is different, and what feels like a 4 to you will be a different speed than a 4 for someone else. The key here is to start paying attention to how these levels feel in your body. Over time, your 4 will get faster.

A couple additional comments about this scale:

If you are already at a 5 when you're walking, you'll do walk/walk intervals. Walk at a 4–5 pace when your training plan says to run, and walk at a 3–4 pace when it says to walk. It's all good, and the important thing is that you get yourself into these training zones rather than hit a certain speed.

The interval ratios suggested in the Cindy and Sarah plans are a starting point. Try to follow them exactly as written but, if necessary, you may tweak them a little. If you're following the Cindy plan and it is not challenging you, switch to the Sarah plan. If this still feels too easy, and you're maintaining a 5 throughout your run intervals, increase the duration of the each run interval by 15 seconds to see if that gives you more challenge. Continue to increase by 15 seconds as needed until the workout becomes more difficult to complete. Not impossible, just requiring more effort than before.

Conversely, if you're doing the Cindy plan and the length of the run intervals is too long for you to complete, reduce them by 15 seconds at a time until you are able to complete them at a 5.

Using the RPE scale will help you judge your effort so you know whether you're pushing too hard, not hard enough, or just right.

So, what does this have to do with breathing? Well, when you're at a 7, 8, 9, or 10, your lungs won't be able to keep up with the amount of oxygen that your body needs. This is what results in feeling completely out of breath. Staying in that 4–6 zone means you'll be working hard, but not so hard that you can't keep it up. Your breathing will be faster, but not out of control.

Another way to think about it is to make sure you can easily carry on a short conversation while you're running, without feeling like you can't get the words out. If you can recite the Gettysburg address with no problem (assuming you can remember it), you're going too slow. If answering yes or no questions is difficult, you're going too fast. Adjust accordingly.

Finally, think about taking deeper, longer inhales and exhales. If you are running so fast that you can only take short, shallow breaths, you need to slow down. Running at a 5 means you can inhale over two steps and exhale over two. Getting into that rhythm will help you assess your effort level.

It may take some time for you to become familiar with the RPE scale and how it applies to you. That's totally normal. After a while, it will feel like second nature.

Running form

Everyone's body is different, from the length of your legs and torso, to the way your joints are put together, to how your body fat is distributed. No two people are exactly alike, which means there is no perfect running form that will work for everybody.

I've seen some pretty wacky runners in my travels, some folks with such crazy running form that you wonder how on earth they get from point A to point B without hurting themselves. However, just because it looks odd doesn't mean it's wrong, and if you're able to run more injury-free while breaking some of the cardinal rules of running form, well, I'd say if it ain't broke, don't fix it. And I promise you don't look as silly as you think you do when you're running.

If you believe you run like a gazelle, you will.

That being said, there are some general guidelines which I think will help you become a stronger, injury-free runner. The key is to develop an efficient running form that will use the minimum amount of energy to keep you moving forward.

Feet and legs

If you search the internet, there are dozens of websites telling you not to land on your heel and just as many saying it doesn't matter. I'm in the "it doesn't matter unless you're getting injured" camp.

In general, I recommend aiming to have your feet land directly under your hips when you run (look in your training plan for cues). This means taking shorter steps, but it results in a lighter landing, and allows your leg muscles to do the shock absorption rather than your knee joints. If you carry any extra weight, this is especially important.

One way to know if you're landing with your feet under your hips is to look straight down while running. If you can see your toes peeking out in front of your body, you're doing great. If you can see your entire heel, you're landing too far in front. Shorten your stride. It might feel unnatural at first, but when you get used to taking shorter steps you'll build up lots of strength in your calves, which will really assist you as you start running longer and longer distances. It also helps you avoid the dreaded shin splints.

Keep your feet low to the ground with each step. Bounding forward like a gazelle may look like fun, but it uses a lot of energy. Conserve your resources for forward motion, and you'll go farther.

Torso and head

Keep your body upright. It's easy to slump forward a bit from the shoulders, especially if your core muscles (abs, back and chest) are weak. Over time, this can degrade your running form resulting in backaches and overcompensating in your hips—and compressing your chest cavity which squeezes your lungs and reduces their capacity to take full, deep breaths.

You can help yourself "run tall" by ensuring your head is up, gaze resting about 20-30 feet ahead. When your eyes are constantly looking straight down at the trail, your head and neck will follow and soon you'll be running all hunched over. Focus on looking for obstacles in the distance instead of immediately in front of you.

Do a little form check every few minutes, to make sure your shoulder blades are pulled back, your head is forward, and your torso is upright. You could even imagine a string coming off the top of your head pulling your whole body upwards. This will eventually create the habit of running that way all the time.

Arms

Your arms can either help you or hinder you when running. Pumping them back and forth, like you may have seen during Olympic sprints, is a hindrance. For beginners, this is wasted energy. Keep your elbows bent at a 90-degree angle, hands loose (clenching your fists—you guessed it—wastes energy), and allow your arms to move loosely back to front when you run. Their job is to counterbalance the opposite foot and help you, ever so slightly, with forward momentum. That's it. Otherwise, they're in the way.

WEEK 2 HOMEWORK

You're ready to roll on your Week 2 training plan. Remember to use the RPE scale and keep yourself in that 4–6 range, and I'll see you in week 3!

PUT IT INTO PRACTICE

Cindy started out running the way she thought the Kenyans run: as fast as possible, taking long strides and pumping her arms. She quickly found out that this took so much energy that she was exhausted after about 20 seconds. Then she began telling herself a story that she was not meant to be a runner, and thought about quitting.

Fortunately, she tried the efficient running form described above, and by adjusting her stride to be much shorter and low to the ground, and slowing her pace to a sustainable level, she was able to finish her workout and felt great about it.

The key takeaway from Cindy's experience is that just because one thing doesn't work for you, it doesn't mean you're a failure. It just means you need to modify things until you find what does work.

R: RESOURCEFUL RUNNING
WEEK 3 OF TRAINING

You're in Week 3 and still going strong—way to go! Now that you've mastered intervals, the RPE scale and your mindset, it's time to think about how to handle unexpected situations that might interfere with your run. Becoming a resourceful runner is key to making that happen.

So, what exactly does resourceful mean? According to thesaurus.com: Active, adventurous, bright, capable, creative, enterprising, ingenious, intelligent, inventive, talented.

In other words, all the qualities you already have, right?

Each week you have three running workouts to complete. Even with the best of planning, things will occasionally go awry. Sometimes you can salvage the situation, and sometimes you need to make other plans.

Using the guidelines below, do the best you can to make sure you get your run done. If you absolutely can't do it, a power walk or elliptical session will burn calories and get your heart rate up—but it is not equivalent to a run. Each workout on your training plan plays an important part in your success. So, if worse comes to worst and your run is not happening that day, make sure you reschedule for another day instead of substituting something else.

General Advice

Basic preparedness can head off a ton of emergencies. Think like a Boy Scout:

- Always keep spares of everything in your car and/or gear bag. This includes headphones, socks, hairbands, sports bras, etc. Basically, anything that could result in you not running.

- Keep a first aid kit in your car if you run outdoors and not near your home. This is especially important if you're at a trail and take a spill that breaks the skin. A basic kit should include antibacterial wipes, ointment, and sterile dressing. A roll of paper towels never hurts either.

- Check the weather when you're planning your runs for the next few days. If you know there's a 100% chance of thunderstorms tomorrow, you have plenty of time to make alternate plans. If you're in the dark about what's coming, you'll be in for a wet run.

Gear Mishaps

Sometimes, despite the best planning (see Chapter 1 for the list of how to be prepared), things go wrong. Batteries mysteriously don't charge. The extra 17 hairbands usually floating around the bottom of your gym bag have gone missing. Your sports bra rips and the girls are flapping in the wind. One of your shoes fell out of your bag in the driveway and you don't notice until you're at the gym.

When things like this happen, I usually evaluate what to do based on these criteria:

1. How badly I want/need to run that day.

2. How easy it will be to fix the issue or just run with it.

3. Whether I can reschedule for later (or substitute another activity).

For example, if I've forgotten my ponytail holder, it means I'll probably have to run with my hair getting in my eyes, unless I can find a visor, headband or a hat somewhere (pro tip: always keep a baggie of ponytail holders in your glove compartment for emergencies). To me, that's not the end of the world and I'd probably just go with it. If I was at the gym, I'd ask for a rubber band at the front desk. Inconvenient and less than ideal, yes. But not something that will interfere enough to make me reschedule or skip entirely.

A torn sports bra? For me, that's a show-stopper. I've run in a regular bra once—and *only* once. It was painful, and I actually have a finish line photo with my boobs going in completely different directions (embarrassing, but true). No matter how badly I need to run that day, I'll never, ever run without my Enell again. Power walk? Sure. But not run. It might be different for you, so apply the criteria above to decide.

Here are some examples of how to salvage unfortunate situations:

No running shoes: If you forgot your running shoes, you can do a short run in other sneakers, if you have them available. I wouldn't do more than 45 minutes, but it's not the end of the world. Borrowing someone else's shoes isn't the best idea because you might end up with blisters. But all is not lost—you can do strength training instead! In fact, doing things like squats, lunges, calf raises, etc.—classic moves for runners—is actually more effective in bare or sock feet, because you're engaging all the muscles in your feet and ankles, making them stronger. A strong runner is more likely to be an injury-free runner.

Dead or forgotten phone/GPS/interval timer/iPod: In my humble opinion, you can run without any of these things. It's not ideal, but it shouldn't hold you back. In fact, once in a while it's actually a good idea to run "naked" so that you can reconnect with yourself instead of distracting. Sure, you won't know how far or fast you went, and you may have to estimate your intervals instead of knowing precisely when to switch. But if the choice is *not* running vs. running *without technology*, I'll choose the latter any day. Same goes for music. It can be super-motivating to have your favorite tunes blasting in your ear, but developing the skill of running without it can be really helpful—especially if you're planning to enter a race where headphones aren't allowed.

All the treadmills at the gym are taken and there's a line of 20 people waiting, but all the ellipticals are empty: If you go to the gym at peak times, treadmill availability might be limited. If you can't wait for one to open up, it's time to run laps around the parking lot or head to a local neighborhood. You might be tempted to hit up the elliptical instead, but it's not the best substitute for running, because there is no impact. Your feet never leave the machine's surface. The best way to train for any race is to do the activity you'll be doing on race day. Since you're not doing a 5K on the elliptical, aside from improving your general fitness, it doesn't get you any closer to your training goals. I'd rather see you do 20 minutes on the treadmill than 40 minutes on the elliptical. If you do choose the elliptical so that you can get some sort of exercise, make sure to reschedule your run for another day.

Forgotten water/snack: This is not a show-stopper. You can do 45 minutes of exercise without fuel (it's kind of like running first thing in the morning before breakfast, after you've been sleeping all night). Unless you're coming off a two-day fast, you should probably just go for it. Make sure you get something to eat and drink afterwards and you'll be fine. That being said, listen to your body during your workout. If you feel light-headed or dizzy, it might be time to stop.

Chafing and Blisters

Chafing is the bane of every runner's existence, not just those that are overweight. Those angry, raised, red patches of skin that show up on your body after a long, sweaty run can be really painful, especially when you gratefully hit the showers and the soap hits those raw spots. Blisters can be even more painful and could stop you from running completely, so it's important to make sure you do everything possible to prevent them.

Often, chafing can be avoided by wearing running gear that fits properly, but it's likely it will still happen to you at some point. Fortunately, there are many products to help you prevent this uncomfortable problem. Look for shirts and tights with flat seams—especially between the thighs—and socks with minimal or no seams.

Bodyglide—quite possibly the best thing ever invented after cupcakes—is an anti-chafing substance that looks a little like stick deodorant. Once applied, it feels completely dry, and is invisible, odorless, and water-resistant. Apply it where seams tend to irritate your skin, where you have skin-to-skin contact, or on those places on your feet that tend to rub against your shoes. You won't even know it's there, except when you undress after your run and realize you don't have angry red patches anywhere on your body! There are other products that have similar effects, but in my experience Bodyglide is the best. Avoid Vaseline or any other petroleum jelly. Yes, it will reduce friction. It will also stain your clothes and feel sticky.

Moleskin is an adhesive felt-like material that sticks to your skin and provides a thicker barrier against friction than Bodyglide. It is commonly used on the feet, but you can use it wherever you feel you need extra protection. For example, whenever I use my iPhone armband, the edge of the strap rubs the inside of my arm raw. I place a small piece of moleskin right where the strap hits, and *voila*! Problem solved. It can be cut to any size and removed easily when your workout is done. If you're in a pinch and don't have any moleskin, a band-aid or athletic tape will work.

But what do you do if you end up with chafing or blisters despite all your precautions?

Blisters

In general, you should not pop them, unless they are really large. Cover them with a sterile dressing or an adhesive bandage made specifically for blisters (they usually have extra cushioning) and allow them to resolve on their own. If the blister is really big and uncomfortable, I recommend seeing a medical professional to get it tended to. I know you'll probably be tempted to pop it yourself and that's your call...but your doctor will be able to do it properly.

Chafing

A pain-relieving ointment or petroleum jelly will help with the discomfort, along with a bandage that keeps a friction barrier against clothing. Other than that, there's not much that can be done aside from waiting it out and not further irritating the area.

The Weather

If you're not a treadmill runner, sooner or later you'll need to figure out how to deal with Mother Nature. Cold, heat, rain, snow, fog...depending on where you live, some or all of these conditions will threaten your run. But you're a resourceful runner, which means it doesn't have to slow you down!

Personally, the height of summer is my least favorite time to run. The human body relies primarily on evaporation of sweat to dissipate heat and keep your core temperature properly regulated. In perfect running conditions—60 degrees and about 40% humidity—this is an awesome cooling system. You might not even notice yourself perspiring, and your lungs are breathing in cool, dry air which helps keep you cool from the inside.

However, turn up the heat and/or the humidity, and suddenly the sweat on your skin doesn't evaporate as efficiently, which means your core temperature will start to rise. In addition, the more you sweat, the less blood volume you have. That water has to come from somewhere, and one of the sources is your blood. The lower your blood volume, the less oxygen is available to your muscles, which means it will feel much harder to run the hotter it gets outside.

This doesn't mean you need to completely stop running in the summer, just follow the advice below when it's hot out:

- Run early in the morning or late in the evening, when the temperatures are lower.

- Slow down and take some extra walk breaks. If you normally cover a mile in 14 minutes when the temperature is sixty degrees and dry, you might do a 16-minute mile on a humid, eighty-degree day. **This is normal, and doesn't mean you're getting slower**.

- Expose yourself. The more skin you have uncovered, the easier it will be to keep cool. This means sleeveless tops, and tights that don't go past your knees.

- Wear a lightweight headband or a visor to keep sweat out of your eyes. Avoid hats, which trap heat.

- Don't apply sunscreen above your eyebrows. If you do this, you'll end up with sunscreen *in* your eyes, guaranteed.

- Drink water. Carrying a bottle with you while you run can be a hassle, so leave it next to a fencepost or a tree you'll pass by more than once on your route. If my stash-spot is in a high-traffic area, I usually tape a note to my bottle that says, "Please don't take me. My owner is out running right now and is really looking forward to drinking me later!"

- Put ice cubes in your bra at the start of your run. (I'm serious.)

- If you find yourself overheating, dump water over your head. This is a really fast way to cool down.

- If you have asthma or another respiratory condition, always bring your inhaler and/or take your meds.

- If you suffer from allergies, don't run on high pollen days. The best time to run is right after a rainstorm so that airborne allergens are at a minimum.

- And finally, know the warning signs of heatstroke: chills, dizziness, muscle cramps, weakness and nausea. Always carry your phone in case you need to call for help.

Winter running is also a challenge, but still completely possible. Again, it's all about heat management. Even if it's really cold when you start your run, after a few minutes of running your body temperature will rise and your thick coat will trap your body heat and sweat and it will feel just like running in the middle of summer. To avoid this scenario, dress yourself in light layers—especially on top—so that you can peel them off as your body warms up. One strategy I like to use is to leave my house with a jacket, run for five minutes or so until I'm warmed up, then swing back by my house and drop the jacket off in the mailbox. If it's really cold, I'll wear a second pair of knee-length tights over my full-length tights to help keep my quadriceps muscles warm. Don't forget about water, either. Dry, winter air causes your sweat to evaporate quickly, which means you'll need to replenish your fluids often.

No matter where you live, if you run outdoors, eventually it will rain, snow, hail, or something else when you are running or planning to.

There's no real reason not to run in the rain, unless there's lightning, hail, or flash flooding in the area, but it can be uncomfortable if you're not prepared. You won't find too many waterproof running jackets on the market, because if it keeps water off your body, it also traps any moisture you generate which can lead to overheating and chafing. So if you choose to run in the rain or snow, plan on getting wet.

On really wet days, slip a plastic baggie over your socks before you put your shoes on to keep your feet dry. Use extra BodyGlide on your feet and other body parts prone to chafing, and make sure to put your electronics in a waterproof case (or a Ziploc baggie). Keep an extra close eye on traffic, too—wet or icy roads can be slippery so stick to routes where you'll be far from moving vehicles.

Running in the snow is amazing. Packed snow or a shallow layer of fluffy snow is ideal, because it has traction and cushioning. It feels good on the feet and if you're lucky enough to be running while it's snowing, there's this lovely hush that falls when all the sounds in the world are muffled by the falling snow. I love it. But if the snow turns to ice, it's best to hit up the treadmill instead. You could try putting little spikes on your shoes, but sometimes that can interfere with your gait or make things uncomfortable. For your first training program, I'd play it safe and run indoors when it's icy outside.

Dogs

I love, love, love dogs. In fact, I used to have a greyhound named Lola. She was beautiful, gentle and a great running companion. But even the most gentle of dogs can snap at you when they're startled. So, if you're out running and you come across a dog—either on a leash or not—be wary of approaching it until you can assess its body language. Move out of the way, and don't attempt to interact without asking the owner first. If the dog is wandering about without its human, just don't approach it at all. A dog bite is painful, and requires treatment if the skin is broken. Avoidance is the best policy.

If you are bitten, make sure to get the owner's name and address in case there are complications down the road (or take a picture of the dog if you can't find the owner nearby). You'll also want to ensure the dog has a current rabies shot. If not, it could result in a very painful treatment for you.

Injuries

Injuries will happen. You might step off a curb wrong and turn your ankle, run face first into a low hanging branch, or try some fancy dance moves on the treadmill and end up on the floor.

In general, if you get hurt while you're running and you're unable to continue without pain, stop, walk home or back to your car if you can (or call someone for a ride if not), and then follow basic first aid techniques or visit your urgent care clinic. Always keep a first-aid kit in your car for simple treatments.

If you're running at the gym and hurt yourself, contact gym staff immediately for help. Let them know what happened, because they will need to make a report, and, depending on the situation, they might be responsible if you require medical assistance as a result of the incident. When in doubt, let them know.

Basically, use common sense. I'd rather see you cut your run short than further injure yourself—but if you can keep going, you might as well finish!

WEEK 3 HOMEWORK

Get busy on your week 3 training plan. Why not take a chance on a new running route this week? If you're a tread-mill runner, try running in your neighborhood instead. And, as always, remember to use the RPE scale and keep yourself in that 4–6 range. See you in week 4!

PUT IT INTO PRACTICE

This week, Sarah forgot to charge her phone on the way to her daughter's school and she found herself without music and a timer. Since this was her designated running time, she didn't want to reschedule but she also didn't want to spend the entire workout looking at her digital watch while she was running, and calculating when it was time to stop. She warmed up by walking to a nearby neighborhood and improvised as follows:

Using her watch, she timed herself running the first interval and noticed how many driveways she passed. Then she counted the driveways on the walk interval. Using these numbers, she counted driveways for each interval so that she could stop worrying about looking at her watch. It turned out to be really fun, and she also found herself really paying attention to her breathing and how her body felt instead of just zoning out to her music like usual.

F: FUEL
WEEK 4 OF TRAINING

Three weeks down! You're almost to the halfway point now, can you believe it? Now it's time for everyone's favorite chapter—fuel. And by that, I mean keeping your body in peak running condition.

There are two components to fueling yourself for peak performance: hydration and nutrition.

Hydration

Water is the most important nutrient in your body. Every organ and tissue needs it for survival—even your bones. Without enough water, blood thickens and slows down, which means less oxygen for your muscles and other organs. Insufficient water can also impact body temperature, because there will be less sweat to keep you cool. Being slightly dehydrated can result in feeling tired, headachy, slow—and if the problem isn't fixed, you'll end up overheated and possibly even get heatstroke (you really don't want this to happen).

Fortunately, it's really easy to stay hydrated—just drink water! Unless you have a diagnosed electrolyte deficiency, or you're running for more than 2 hours at a time (which in the case of 5K training, you're not), water is the best liquid to keep your body running smoothly. There's no need for sports drinks or supplements.

For the purposes of this 5K program, you won't need to carry a water bottle with you while you run (although you're welcome to do so if you'd like). Why? Because keeping yourself properly hydrated on a regular basis will ensure that your body has enough water to keep you going for 45 minutes to an hour. In addition, carrying a water bottle or hydration pack is an added level of complexity and hassle, and I want to keep things as simple as possible for you during this program to make sure you don't get bogged down and distracted by things that aren't going to improve your performance.

So we're going to focus on techniques to keep your water levels in good shape all the time, and how to properly replace lost fluids *after* your training workouts are complete.

Throughout the day, aim for around 6–8 glasses of water, or if you use one of those big 24 oz water bottles, fill it 3 times. Use your urine as a guide. Pale yellow = hydrated. Dark yellow = dehydrated.

In addition to drinking water, make sure to include lots of unprocessed fruits and veggies in your diet. Did you know that most plants are really high in moisture content? For example, watermelon and strawberries contain approximately 92% water by volume, as do cauliflower, peppers and spinach. Even white potatoes are 82% water. By contrast, bread is around 40%, and pretzels are around 6%.

By the way, the benefit of including unprocessed plant foods as part of your hydration plan is that you also get the bonus of tons of important nutrients and fiber along with the liquid. Win-win!

In my experience, there's no need to drink a ton of water right before you run. A few ounces? Sure. But any more than that and it will just slosh around and probably give you a side stitch. No fun. Better to drink it an hour or two before so it has a chance to absorb.

After your workout, drink at least 16 ounces of water, more if it was an especially hot and sweaty run. The more you sweat, the more you need to replace.

A couple of things to remember: anything containing alcohol or caffeine (such as soda, coffee, energy drinks, or even some teas) acts as a diuretic, which causes your body to release more water than usual. So if you're a regular caffeine or alcohol user, you may need to pay closer attention and drink a little extra water. Again, use the color of your urine as a gauge. When in doubt, check in with your doctor for advice.

Finally, consume alcohol in moderation after any run, and never, ever, drink it before a run. In addition to the dehydrating effect, it also clouds your judgment and impairs your reflexes—which can lead to accidents and injuries (or accidentally spilling all your secrets to your training buddy).

Nutrition

Everyone's bodies are different, and there is no single nutritional plan that fits all. For a 5K run, there is no need for special fueling products, the kind you find in the protein supplement aisle of the supermarket that promise to make you unstoppable. I recommend the same approach to food that I do for water: if you're going to be running for less than 2 hours, your body should be able to get through a 5K workout without needing supplemental fuel half way through. So keep your body properly fueled every day and you'll be fine.

Carbohydrates, protein and fat are all important for runners, at different times. Carbs put gas in the tank, so to speak. That's what your muscles use to help them move, and without carbs, you might as well have a flat tire. That being said, the concept of carbo-loading before a race or run is a myth. Most of us get more than enough carbs on a daily basis to keep the tank full.

I like to follow Michael Pollan's rule of thumb: If your great-grandmother wouldn't recognize it as food, don't eat it. Feed yourself the highest quality fuel possible, at all times. This means avoiding processed foods, eating lots of fruits, vegetables and high quality protein, sticking to complex carbs (rather than highly refined grains and sugar) and—yes, really—including some fat in your diet.

Avoid big meals in the couple of hours before a run. If you're hungry, or running first thing in the morning, have a small snack such as a piece of fruit or a handful of nuts instead. Even then, your muscles should have enough stored fuel to get you through your workout on an empty stomach. Blood flow is diverted away from non-essential organs when you're exercising, to make sure your muscles can be properly supplied with oxygen. This includes your digestive tract. That means any food that isn't quickly and easily absorbed will lie like a rock in your stomach while you run, because your body is busy doing other things. It is no fun to run with a bellyache. It's even less fun to stop running so you can puke.

After your workout, make sure you refuel with both protein and carbohydrates within 30 minutes. It doesn't need to be a lot: a piece of string cheese and some apple slices, or half a banana and some peanut butter, will be enough. The carbs will help your body replace lost energy stores, and the protein is important to help rebuild your muscles after the stress of your workout. Plus, if you don't eat something shortly after your run, you'll find yourself a couple of hours later eating everything that isn't nailed down, and regretting it afterwards. Reward your body for its hard work with a high quality snack and it won't torture you with the "run-gries" that night.

For ideas on pre- and post-run snacks, download a list at my website (www.notyouraveragerunner.com/run-snack-list).

WEEK 4 **HOMEWORK**

Move on to your week 4 training plan, and pay close attention this week to your hydration and nutrition. Consider making a few notes in your journal about it! What you ate before and after, how hydrated you were, and how you felt on your run. If you're struggling a little with energy levels, keeping track of what you're eating and drinking can often pinpoint some areas where you could make some changes and feel better. See you in Week 5!

PUT IT INTO PRACTICE

Cindy found herself struggling a bit with what to eat before her Saturday morning runs. She really didn't like to eat first thing in the morning, so she tried just drinking a cup of coffee before her run and found herself urgently needing to go to the bathroom about 15 minutes into her workout, and her tummy was also upset from the acidity of the coffee sloshing around. This made for a pretty uncomfortable run, so she decided to go running before her morning coffee and try a small amount of food instead.

What ended up working really well for her was about 4 apple slices with a little bit of peanut butter, and a few sips of water. Just enough to settle her stomach a little bit, but not so much that she felt like she had to force-feed herself. She also found that waiting about 20 minutes after eating gave her enough time to digest and she spent that time getting dressed, planning her route and programming her interval timer.

I: INITIATE YOURSELF INTO THE CLUB
WEEK 5 OF TRAINING

You've officially made it to the halfway point! I'm really proud of you and this week it's time to reward yourself with—wait for it—*shopping*!

Now that you've established that you are, in fact, a runner, I'm going to teach you all the secrets of how to look the part. Where to get the best clothes, what shoes to wear, whether you really need that $500 GPS watch, all that great stuff.

It's really easy to spend a fortune on running gear that seemed like a good idea at the time, but mostly just ends up in a pile under your bed or at the back of the closet after a couple of uses. Hopefully, this chapter will help you avoid some of those mistakes, and save you some cash along the way.

The first lesson? (Warning—tough love ahead!) Stop using your clothes to hide your body when you run, and quit worrying about what others think. Nobody else is even looking at you while you run, thinking about how fat your arms look in that tank top, or whether your running tights show too much (unless you're wearing white running tights in which case, just... don't). The truth is, most people are far too concerned about themselves to look at anyone else for more than a passing glance. Unless you're dressed like a unicorn and singing along to John Denver at the top of your lungs, nobody cares.

When it comes to workout clothes, and running gear in particular, wearing stuff that fits properly is critical. Why? Because if it isn't comfortable, your run will suck. You'll either be messing around with your clothes the whole time, trying to adjust them to feel right, or you'll be so miserable that you'll quit early. We don't want that to happen. So trust me, invest in gear that fits the size you are right now. If you lose inches in a couple of months, you can get new clothes for not much money, I promise.

The key pieces of gear that you need are *tights, tops, sports bra, hat/visor, running shoes, wicking socks, and reflective vest.* Make sure you have duplicates of everything so that you never have to skip a run because something is in the laundry.

The ideal material for running gear (including undies!) is a light, soft, seamless synthetic blend that draws moisture away from your skin and dries quickly. CoolMax, DryMax and QuikWik are common fabrics, but you can also get away with Spandex, Lycra, or a blend. Check labels and make sure anything you purchase has little to no cotton. Cotton traps sweat, which can lead to a pretty miserable workout.

Your gear will last longer if you take good care of it. Always wash in cold water, and never, ever put them in the dryer. Heat breaks down Spandex and Lycra, shortening their lifespan. Hang them on a rack when they come out of the washer, and they'll be ready to wear in a few hours.

Remember, sweaty clothes start to smell pretty bad after a few days, so don't let them sit in a dark, closed hamper until it's time to do laundry. If you can't wash them within a day, make sure to put them in an open basket, which will allow them to dry. And if you do find that your gear has an odor, soak it in a vinegar solution for a few hours and rewash.

Tops And Bottoms

If you dress like a runner, you'll feel like a runner. Get yourself suited up properly and something magical happens: you look in the mirror and see a real runner. And it doesn't have to cost an arm and a leg, either. Nowadays, there are tons of cost-effective and cute options in sizes up to 4X, in places that just might surprise you.

Get a free roundup of the best places to get plus-size running gear, including size ranges, price ranges, shipping and return policies, at my website (www.notyouraverage runner.com/gear-guide). If you wear yoga pants, loose shorts, or sweatpants to run, you leave yourself open to chafing from the seams between your thighs. Anything that doesn't hug your legs is going to ride up, which means you'll spend a lot of time tugging them back down.

Running tights may not leave much to the imagination. I get it. Sometimes it can feel like your body is on display. But they are actually designed to make running easier and more comfortable by reducing friction, chafing, wind resistance, and even helping keep your wobbly bits under control. Also, since pretty much everyone is wearing them nowadays, you'll look a lot more out of place running in baggy yoga pants than you will in proper running tights.

Of course, if you're still feeling over-exposed, consider a running skirt, which combines tights with a skirt that hangs to mid-thigh. They come in lots of fun colors, too!

Running tops are also made to reduce friction and chafing. Feel free to hide behind enormous cotton t-shirts, but not only do you look like a first-timer, you'll be pretty uncomfortable once you start sweating and the moisture is trapped under your huge shirt. Do yourself a favor, drop the security blanket and rock your curves! Wear a short-sleeved shirt, or (gasp!) a tank top in the hot months. I *promise* that nobody is looking at your arms. You'll feel much more confident as a runner if you are comfortable.

Sports Bra

When you run, your breasts move up and down as well as side to side. For those of you that have A and B cups, this is mostly just an inconvenience. But if you're a C cup or more, all of that extra motion *hurts*. It is uncomfortable while you run, and over time can cause back pain and even throw your gait out of whack, which can result in even more issues.

A good sports bra will effectively immobilize your breasts while you're running, so there is almost no movement whatsoever. It can change everything, making it so much easier to run that you might almost forget you have boobs at all.

Proper support isn't cheap, but if you invest in two or three well-made bras and take good care of them, they will last you for years. Choose one made primarily from a synthetic blend (with little to no cotton) that doesn't have much too much stretch (stretch equals bounce), and make sure it is rated as a motion-control bra. Padded, wide straps are best for larger breasts, while smaller girls can get away with racerback, pullover styles. Get measured (or follow the instructions on the website) to make sure you're getting the right size. If you're spilling out of it everywhere, this defeats the purpose. More coverage means more control.

In my opinion, the best choice is the Enell Sport. They were created for active women that are a C cup or larger, and provide more support than any other running bra on the market. They also come in cute colors and last forever, and if you don't quite fit into the standard sizes they offer, you can get one custom-made to fit you perfectly. A one-time investment of roughly $65 dollars and you'll have a bra that'll last for five years or longer. They're that good.

Shoes and Socks

Choosing the perfect running shoe is not easy, and it may take you a couple of tries to get it right. What works well for your best friend might be a terrible choice for you. Everyone's biomechanics are different, and there are too many factors at play to recommend one shoe or brand over another. Visit your local running store and have them measure your feet, analyze your gait, and discuss your weekly mileage and typical running surfaces before making a recommendation.

A reputable store will allow you to run a short distance in the shoes, perhaps around the parking lot or on a treadmill in the store, and they absolutely must accept returns, at a minimum for store credit. Running shoes are not cheap, and you can expect to pay $100 or more for a good pair, so make sure you have the option to exchange them if they are not working for you. Ask a lot of questions, and understand the store policies before you buy. Online merchants, such as RoadRunnerSports.com, have incredibly generous return policies, great prices and a huge selection.

For most people, socks are an afterthought, but they're actually pretty important. If they are too big or too small, too thick or too thin, you can end up with blisters. If possible, choose socks with little to no cotton, and plan to try a few different styles until you get it right.

Visibility

Unless your running is all done on a treadmill, safety gear is something you need to understand— especially if you're running anywhere near traffic. People are distracted behind the wheel. It sucks, but it's true. Therefore, visibility to oncoming drivers is critical. Choose at least one piece of clothing—top or bottom—that is brightly colored and has a reflective logo or stripe. At dawn, dusk and after dark—

anytime drivers have their headlights on—use reflective vests or arm/ankle bands. Blinking lights are another excellent way to make sure you're seen. Basically, anything that draws attention to your presence on the side of the road is good.

If you're running in a poorly lit area after dark, use a small headlamp to see where you're going. Finally, always carry ID with you, either a driver's license or an identifying wristband (such as RoadID) with your name, emergency contact, and medical alerts.

Gadgets and Other Fun Stuff

This is where running can start to get really expensive. You can spend upwards of $500 on a high-end GPS watch. Fortunately, you really don't need to. Use a free smartphone app such as RunKeeper to track your distance, and a $20 interval timer to count off your intervals (I love the GymBoss), and you really don't need anything else. Keeping it simple also has another benefit—fewer barriers to getting yourself out the door. As long as your phone is charged, you're ready to go. The bonus of using a smartphone app? You can easily post your stats to Facebook to impress (or annoy) your friends.

That being said, lots of things can help enhance your experience. Nowadays, manufacturers are adding thoughtful details to their clothing lines, such as waistband key pockets, or chest pockets specifically designed to hold a smartphone. When you're shopping, look for things like holes for headphones, built-in pockets for a phone and extra-long sleeves with thumbholes to keep your hands warm in the winter.

If you don't want to carry a smartphone while you run, but still want the benefits of GPS, a GPS watch might be the answer. You can get one for as little as $100 if all you want is mileage. After you run, stats are downloaded to your computer so you can review them with ease.

WEEK 5 HOMEWORK

Move on to your Week 5 training plan, and start shopping around for some new running gear. Step outside your comfort zone with some new colors and styles, and see if this changes how you feel about yourself when you're running. See you in Week 6!

PUT IT INTO PRACTICE

One of Sarah's biggest challenges was seeing herself as a runner. She noticed that all of the coaches in her daughter's Girls on the Run program wore really brightly colored tights and tops, and she envied how cute their gear was. Even after losing 124 pounds, Sarah still felt frumpy and was constantly trying to hide the body she'd worked so hard to get.

One day, she and her daughter were out shopping and saw a pair of bright purple tights with a starburst pattern on them. They were definitely something one of the coaches would wear and Sarah was instantly drawn to them. Before she knew it, she'd put them in her shopping cart and bought them.

Later at home, she tried them on for her daughter who absolutely loved them. This was the first time Sarah had ever worn anything to draw attention to her body, but she had to admit, when she looked at herself in the mirror, she kinda liked what she saw! The compression of the tights made her butt look awesome, and the color was just so fun that it was hard not to smile. She decided to wear them on her next run and after getting compliments from one of her daughter's coaches, she got the confidence to buy another pair, along with a matching top.

R: RESILIENT RUNNER
WEEK 6 OF TRAINING

Running is a repetitive motion sport. One foot in front of the other, over and over again, always in the same direction. As a result, runners are prone to overuse injuries and tightness in the large muscles used for running (such as quads, glutes, calves and hamstrings). The truth is, at some point in your running career, you'll probably get injured. It might be a nagging pain in your left knee that you can take care of with some physical therapy and a knee brace, or it could be a sprained ankle from stepping off a curb the wrong way. I can honestly say I don't know a single runner who hasn't had some sort of issue that was a result of running.

If this sounds like bad news, it's not. Of all those runners I mentioned above, I also can't think of a single one who has permanently stopped running as a result of their injuries.

Injuries are a pain in the neck. Many of you will be lucky; your issues will be mild and resolve quickly with a little rest and ice. Unfortunately, a few of you will need to deal with the annoyance of taking a longer break from your running routine. This is the unhappy truth, but it doesn't mean you are doomed to fail.

In all my years of running, I've had a lot of injuries. Achilles tendinitis, patellar tendinitis, plantar fasciitis, shin splints, bruised toes, IT band issues, osteoarthritis. You name it, it seems like I've had it, and managed my way through it. The main lesson I've learned? Injuries heal if you let them. The problem is, taking the time to let them heal can be a big challenge.

Pain is your body's way of telling you it needs attention. Your body is smart! Listen to what it says, and learn the difference between discomfort, the voice of your inner mean girl and actual pain. You can run through discomfort and the negative voices in your head, but nine times out of ten you should not run through pain.

When you think you're injured, or have a chronic pain that just won't go away, do your research. There are countless resources available online or in books. Ask other runners or stop by your local running store. One of best books on becoming an injury-free runner is *Running Strong*, by Jordan Metzl. He explains the mechanics of running and injuries in detail so you understand exactly what's going on with your specific condition.

Please remember that reading a book on injuries is not a substitute for seeing a specialist in person and getting a professional opinion. A book will help you understand what's going on, but you should never self-diagnose. Make an appointment with an orthopedist and tell that person everything about your pain. Get the MRI, the x-rays, or any other recommended tests. Do the physical therapy exactly as prescribed.

If you don't get relief, seek a second opinion. It's your body. Nobody else will care as much about getting you out of pain as you. It's extremely important that you become your own advocate and speak up if your injury is not resolved! Another doctor might have a different approach to treatment that works for you. Don't stop asking questions until you get the right answer.

Recovery from any injury almost always requires rest. *Active* rest is usually prescribed, which means refraining from running but doing other activities such as cycling or swimming. Forcing yourself to take a break from running is not always easy. It's likely that your routine is working for you, and you might be afraid that taking a break will cause you to lose your motivation and never get back on track. A lot of women feel angry, frustrated, and defeated—which is a perfect opportunity for your inner mean girl to step up, telling you that your body has betrayed you, that you've failed yet again, and that you'll never be a real runner.

Here's the thing. To your inner mean girl, there's no difference between rest and quitting. But she's totally wrong! Quitting is a result of giving up hope, not believing in yourself, thinking that you're a failure so why even try. Rest is a result of loving yourself and your body, believing it deserves the best care possible, and wanting to set yourself up for success so you can be a runner for the next twenty-plus years.

While you're training for your 5K, it's unlikely that you'll end up with a significant injury, especially if you follow the interval progressions in your training plan. The reason I recommend only running three times per week is to give your body a chance to slowly adapt to running, and allow plenty of time for rest. When you're a beginner, and are excited about running, it's tempting to want to do more. I totally get it, but holding yourself back in the beginning will allow you to do more in the long term.

This week you're going to start stretching after each workout. You may have been doing this all along, which is awesome. However, I haven't talked about stretching prior to this point because I wanted to get you in the habit of running without overwhelming you with too much information. Now that you have an established routine, it's time to add a little more.

Stretching should be done so that you feel sensation in the target muscle group—but never pain. Make sure that you are able to hold on to something stable (such as a wall or the back of a chair) for any stretches that are done while standing. Trying to balance on one leg while stretching the other means you won't be able to give 100% of your attention and effort to the stretch because you'll be worried about falling over. It can also lead to injury if you are twisting your body around to keep your balance. Save the balance work for yoga class.

Do your stretches after you've completed your run (not before), while your muscles are still warm. Your training plan this week contains a basic routine that will ensure all your key muscle groups are included. It shouldn't take more than 5 minutes and you might even find out that you like it!

WEEK 6 HOMEWORK

Move on to your Week 6 training plan, and make sure to schedule an extra 5 minutes for your stretches. If you have any developing pains during or after your run, make an appointment with a sports doctor to get it checked out. See you in Week 7!

PUT IT INTO PRACTICE

Cindy has been feeling pain in her shins when she runs. It goes away after about 15 minutes, and she's been working really hard to follow proper form, but the shin pain keeps bothering her.

She wears high heels a lot, which tends to tighten up those muscles, and this can contribute to shin splints. This week, she started stretching her calves thoroughly after each run, as well as once or twice a day while she's at work. She also started adding a few extra minutes to her warmup walk. After a few days, she began to notice that her shin pain was slightly less intense, so she has been keeping up with it—and finding that as long as she stretches regularly, her shin pain is minimal.

S: STAY MOTIVATED
WEEK 7 OF TRAINING

Can you believe that you've been training for six weeks already? There's only two weeks left in your training plan and then it's time to race!

So why are we talking about motivation, now that you're clearly a runner, destined for greatness? Because believe it or not, this is the most common time for people to quit—right when everything is going perfectly. Up until now, you've been excited about your new activity, watching yourself get stronger and faster with each workout. But eventually the newness wears off and there's no excitement left to keep you going, which is why we need to bring in some additional techniques.

Conventional wisdom teaches that it takes 21 days to create a new habit. That might be true for things like nail biting or knuckle-cracking, but in my experience, creating new health habits takes a lot longer than 3 weeks. You can always white-knuckle your way through a few weeks, but as soon as your willpower gets used up, you're left wondering where your mojo went.

And if it really were as easy as doing something for 3 weeks, almost everyone who says they want to lose weight would be thin already, right? The truth is, building a running habit involves a lot more than just doing something different for a few weeks until the habit takes hold.

You've got a lot more to overcome than just substituting one activity for another. For example, sipping water every time you want to bite your nails is a pretty easy switch. The barrier to creating that new habit is really low, because it is just as easy to keep a bottle of water nearby and remember to take a sip every time the urge to nibble on your cuticles comes up.

Building a habit that requires equal measures of learning something new (how to run properly), giving something up (30-40 minutes of relaxing) and doing something hard (the physical challenges of pushing yourself out of your comfort zone) takes quite a bit of mental and physical effort. The barrier to entry is high.

Right now, you've got your 5K goal pulling you forward, but soon your race will be behind you—so now is the time to start connecting with the deeper reasons that you run, because these are the things that will help you stick with it over time.

Remember those counter-proposals we talked about in your prep week? It's time to strengthen them and create even more. We do this by clearly understanding the benefits that running gives you. Not just on an intellectual level, but getting it deep inside your mind.

One of the easiest and most powerful ways to know how running benefits you is to take notes, before and after your runs, in order to document the changes. This week, I want you to take an extra couple of minutes before and after each workout to capture this information:

- Record how your body feels before your run, then after. If you were feeling tired and sluggish beforehand, do you feel energized afterwards?

- What about your emotions? Did your run take you from agitated to relaxed? Sad to happy? Dejected to optimistic? Frustrated to peaceful?

- Try to choose at least two body sensations and two emotions before, and two of each afterwards, to document what running can do for you.

- Next, write about some of the other changes you're seeing in your body and life—such as how cool it feels to realize you can run farther and faster than before, or how awesome it is when you realize you've gone running three times a week for six weeks straight—longer than you've ever stuck with an exercise program before.

- Now, what other evidence can you find to remind you of your success? Are people calling you a runner, or asking you how they can get started? Make sure you write down every time this happens, so you can refer back to it on days when you don't feel like a runner.

I remember the day someone stopped me in the hall at work, when I still weighed almost 250 pounds, and said

"You're a runner, right? Can you help me figure out some stretches to do after my runs? I need some expert advice."

Whoa. That was quite a moment for me. I didn't look like a runner, but I'd been doing it so consistently and with such confidence that other people just assumed I knew what I was talking about.

The reality of running, or anything that you do with regularity, is that some days you just won't feel like it. It's completely normal. Even Olympic athletes have days where they'd rather hang out on the couch with a bag of Doritos than do one more 4-hour sprint workout.

The difference is that they expect to have those days, and they are prepared with counter-proposals and other ammunition to get themselves to the track, the pool or the tennis court, because pursuing their long-term goal is more important than a few moments of feeling good by skipping their workout.

When you feel the pull of wanting an extra 30 minutes of sleep in the morning (assuming you have gotten at least 6-7 hours already) or the lure of watching reruns of *Friends* after work instead of doing your workout, remember all of the things you journaled about.

Decide what you want more—completing your first 5K, or an extra hour on the couch. Is the short term feel-good distraction more important than the long term goal? Will you regret not going for a run when you wake up tomorrow morning?

Know the answers to these questions and it will be a lot easier to get yourself out the door. Or if you decide that an evening on the couch IS more important than running, you've just saved yourself the torture of guilt, because consciously making the decision one way or the other means you've weighed the pros and cons and made an informed choice.

You might have been hoping this chapter would include a long list of tips and tricks to get you out the door on days when you're just not feeling it. I get it. Sometimes it's just easier to have someone else tell you what to do. And trust me, I do have a long list of motivational strategies that I could share.

The problem is, unless you're internally motivated to do it, you won't stick with it for very long. Create your own list and you'll be a lot more successful in the long run.

WEEK 7 HOMEWORK

Move on to your Week 7 training plan, and take some time to write about what felt awesome about each one. Use the journaling prompts if you need to. Make sure to include the before and after feelings, and start creating your own list of motivational strategies. See you in Week 8!

PUT IT INTO PRACTICE

Sarah has a demanding job, and sometimes she is tempted to use her running time to answer emails on her phone while her daughter is at practice. As the primary breadwinner in the family, she worries that taking too much time for herself will impact how she is perceived at work and, ultimately, her salary.

The truth is, by making her health and her relationship with her daughter a priority, she is demonstrating to her coworkers, her boss, and her employees that she is a strong, confident woman who believes that a balanced life is her right as a human being. They have seen the changes in how she carries herself now that she's a runner, and look up to her as a role model.

T: TRY IT OUT
WEEK 8 OF TRAINING

This is it—the final week of training. It's almost go time! You've worked really hard to get to this point and this final week of training is all about setting yourself up for success on race day, so you can run your best race and have fun while you're doing it.

One of the cardinal rules of race day is *never try anything new*. Your training period is not just for building up strength and endurance—it's also for trying out race day strategies such as what to wear and how to eat. This week you'll do a dress rehearsal for the big day—clothes, gadgets, nutrition, and timing—so you can address any potential issues rather than having them crop up during your race. Everything you've practiced for the past 2 months is finally going to come together!

Plan Your Race Day Outfit

By now, you have done enough running that you know which outfits are your favorites, make you feel fabulous, and don't require you to constantly tug on the seams to keep them in place. This is what you should wear on race day. An outfit that will not distract you and frustrate you, that boosts your confidence, and reminds you that you're a real runner.

Prepare a good weather outfit and one that is appropriate for inclement weather (such as longer tights, a jacket and gloves if it's cold). As always, make sure you've tried them out. Before your dress rehearsal, check the expected weather on race day and wear the outfit you think you'll need.

Plan Your Nutrition

A 5K is a short race (even though it might feel long to you). So pre-race nutrition is important, but if you need to run on an empty stomach, it's not the end of the world. What's more important is what you eat and drink in the days leading up to the event. Make sure you stay well hydrated this week. The night before your race, refrain from eating junk food and fuel yourself with high quality nutrition. Again, a 5K is a short race, so there is no need to carb load with a huge plate of pasta. A balanced meal with limited or no alcohol is perfect. Grab a small snack the morning before you run—whatever you've practiced with—and you're good to go.

Race Website

In the weeks leading up to your race, make sure you review all of the website information carefully, as well as any emails you've received. Sometimes these can seem like they're written in a foreign language, and it's easy to just ignore what you don't understand. That could be a big mistake, because they might contain important rules that impact you. Here's a quick guide to the terms you need to know:

Race director: This is the person ultimately responsible for the execution of the event. He or she is the person who makes the decisions.

Race bib: Is also known as your race number. You'll pin it on your shirt. Sometimes there are rules about where it needs to go, make sure you know them. Also, place it so that it can be easily seen while you're running. This helps race officials make sure that everyone on the course is registered, and also helps identify you in race photos.

Race packet: This contains your race bib, timing chip, may include a course map and other instructions. It often has a bunch of coupons and random stuff from sponsors. Sometimes you get lucky and there's free chapstick! You'll usually have to pick up your race shirt at a separate table, after you pick up your packet.

Aid stations: These are tables set up along the course with volunteers giving you water and other sports drinks. For a 5K, there are normally at least two. The volunteers will hand you a cup as you pass by—make sure to ask whether it is water or Gatorade so you don't get any surprises. They will usually have both available.

Timing chip: This is a device that attaches to your shoe or the back of your race number. It detects the exact time you cross the start and finish mats to determine your chip time (see definition below). Unless you're at the very front of the pack, it will take you anywhere from a few seconds to several minutes to get over the starting mat after the starting gun is fired. If you have a timing chip, this period of time is not counted against you. Unless the race you're running is small, or informal, it's likely that you'll have a timing chip provided to you in your race packet. Make sure to read the instructions in your packet, because sometimes you have to return them at the end of the race.

Clock time: The time elapsed between when the starting gun is fired, and when you cross the finish line.

Chip time: The time elapsed between when you cross the starting mat and the finish line (usually shorter than clock time).

Race Expo: If you're doing a 5K that's part of a larger event such as a marathon, you might pick up your packet at the Expo. This is just another way of saying "a huge sports fair" and it's also a chance for vendors to set up booths and try to sell you stuff. You can often get really good deals on discontinued gear, or try new nutrition bars and drinks for free. Just make sure you don't get so distracted by all the fun stuff that you forget to grab your race packet!

Race Rules and Logistics

To make sure you are able to run your best race, it is critical to know the race rules and logistics. I would hate to see you get disqualified for not following a rule that you didn't even know about! Review the race website and familiarize yourself with the information so there are no surprises. Make sure to carefully read any emails the race organizers have sent you. In your training plan this week is a checklist of questions to answer, including:

- Weather policy: what happens if the race is cancelled due to rain?

- Where are the starting and finish lines, and where can your family and friends cheer you on?

- What time do you need to be there?

- Are headphones allowed on the race course?

- Where and when can you pick up your race bib and t-shirt? For many races, you can do this the morning of the event, but large races often require you to pick up your packet the day before.

- What information do you need to bring with you when you pick up your packet? ID? Registration receipt? Can someone else pick it up for you if you're not available?

- Where is race parking, and do you need to have cash on hand to pay for it?

- Will there be any road closures? Does this affect the route you'll be driving to get to the race?

- Where are the aid stations?

- Will you have a timing chip, and will you need to return it after the race?

- If you don't find answers to your questions, email the race director and post the question on the race's Facebook page.

A few miscellaneous tips to remember:

- Make sure not to throw out the pins that come with your race packet. They are for your bib and you will need them.

- Plan to arrive early enough for at least two last minute port-a-potty visits. Trust me on this.

- You will almost always get a race shirt. You may or may not get a finisher's medal for a 5K.

- Pack your stuff and lay out your outfit the night before, so the next morning you can just get up, get dressed, eat your breakfast and go.

- If you're picking up your bib at the race expo, make sure you leave enough time to shop and browse.

After you've planned everything out, do a dress rehearsal of the distance with the gear you plan to use on race day, at roughly the same time of day, and using your intervals and nutrition that you've been training with.

WEEK 8 HOMEWORK

Move on to your Week 8 training plan, and use the checklist to plan out your success strategies. Do your dress rehearsal one week ahead of race day, and make any adjustments you need to make so that your 5K goes smoothly. And don't forget to read the next chapter for guidelines on how to run your actual race!

5K: RACE DAY!

Race day is finally here—time to put all your hard work over the past 2 months to the test! The prep work is complete: your gear is ready, you've worked out all the logistics of getting to the start line, family and friends are waiting at the finish line to cheer you on. All that's left to do is run.

And, of course, I have a few final pieces of advice to help you do it!

It's completely normal to feel nervous the night before the race. Most people don't sleep well, and that's OK. Just get what sleep you can, and know that everyone else is in the same boat.

Your goal is to finish feeling amazing and proud. The time on the clock is irrelevant.

The day of your race is not the time to experiment with a new outfit, new food, or new interval ratios. Stick with what has worked for you throughout your training.

Use the intervals that worked for you during your long training runs. If you felt great with a 1-minute run/1-minute walk ratio, now is not the time to sprint out of the gate and try to run the first 10 minutes. This will tire you out quickly, and you won't have anything left to give in the last mile.

Be patient, start out slow, and save something for that finish line sprint. You want to look happy and energetic for the photographers, not tired and defeated.

The Night Before the Race

- Lay out your clothes and gear—including timing chip, shoes, tights, top, jacket, gloves, socks, undies, sports bra and hat or a headband.

- Prepare a go-bag with lip balm, bobby pins, extra ponytail holder, Bodyglide, contact lens solution, water bottle, granola bar, sunscreen, extra socks, headphones. Every possible thing you think you might need. You can leave it in the car at the last minute, but in the event you need something, you can send someone back to the parking lot to grab it for you.

- Pin your race bib on your shirt, and attach your timing chip if necessary.

- Make sure your morning meal is ready to go.

- Make sure your phone and other devices are charging. Then double check.

- Make sure you know how you're going to carry ID: will it be in a pocket, waist pack or armband? It always helps to stick a credit card and/or a $20 bill in with your ID in case of an emergency.

- Set three alarms, at least one of which is on the other side of the room, so you can't accidentally turn it off.

Make sure to set them for earlier than you think you need to awaken.

- Check the weather one last time.
- Check the race website and your email for any last-minute race announcements.

The Morning of the Race

- Get up earlier than you think you need to. Even if you got everything ready the night before, something always comes up. The dog steals one shoe and hides it. Your phone wasn't fully plugged into the charger and is completely dead.

- Leave earlier than you think you need to. Better to be the first one there and wait around than still parking your car while everyone else is running.

- If no guidance is given on the race site, aim to be at the race location at least 60 minutes before the gun goes off.

Race Day Etiquette

- Place yourself towards the back half of the starting pack and off to one side or the other. There are two reasons for this. First, it's good race etiquette to make sure you're not in the way of faster runners. There is nothing wrong with being slow at all, but just like on a highway, the flow of traffic gets interrupted when slower cars are in the wrong lane.

- After the race starts and the pack thins out, you can run in the center. Just make sure there's plenty of room around you to pass.

- When you pass people, let them know you're on their right or left if you're coming close to them. Nothing is more annoying than having somebody suddenly appear 3 inches away from you when you weren't expecting it.

- Don't follow others too closely. If they stop running, you'll bump right into them. It's actually your responsibility to avoid running into people in front of you, just like in traffic where you shouldn't follow too closely either.

- If you're running with friends, don't run more than 2-3 abreast. Too many people running in a line makes it difficult for others to pass you.

- At the aid stations, take your water and keep moving, so others can get what they need.

- *Selfies*: If you want to take selfies while you're running... please get out of the way of other runners. Unless you want a picture of someone running into your backside!

- Talk to people around you and encourage them! Tell other people they're doing great. be someone's cheerleader, I promise it will make you feel awesome, and it might make the difference between a good and bad race for someone.

- When you get close to the finish line, if you're crossing with other people, try to leave some space in between, otherwise you'll have strangers in your photos (and so will they).

- Wearing the race shirt during the race; this is a hotly debated topic. There are those who staunchly believe that wearing the race shirt is bad karma until you've crossed the finish line (and pretty much shouts to the world you're a newbie). Others wear them with pride. It's really up to you, but remember that wearing a new shirt on race day isn't the best idea simply because you haven't trained in it, which means you could end up not running your best race because your shirt is making you uncomfortable.

After the Race Starts

- Plan to shuffle for a while if there are more than a few hundred people in the race. This is normal, and your chip will take this time into account.

- Remember to follow your intervals from the very beginning!

- Plan to walk the aid stations, so you don't spill water all over the place when you're trying to drink.

- Start a little slower than you think you can maintain for the entire race, and slowly pick up the pace so that you finish the second half faster than the first.

- People will pass you. This is normal and doesn't mean you're running too slowly. Everyone is running his or her own race, and comparing your pace to someone else's is going to dial down your happiness a little.

- There will always be someone older and heavier than you that will leave you in the dust. Look to that person as an example of what is possible, rather than evidence that you suck.

- **Remember, first place and last place both run the same distance!**

- When you see a photographer, smile and wave! This will give you the best chance for awesome race photos.

- As soon as you can see the finish line in the distance, kick yourself into high gear and give it your all!

- Do something fun when you cross the finish line (like my friend Laura who always kicks up her heels)

After You Finish

- Keep your legs moving for at least 20 minutes.

- Drink water, have a snack.

- Hang out around the finish line and cheer other people on.

- Take some time to stretch.

- Take lots of pictures and post them on social media to celebrate! YOU DID IT!

FUTURE FOCUS

Now that you've rocked your first 5K, feeling fabulous and maybe even hanging your race bib on the wall as a reminder of your accomplishment, you're probably wondering what's next. Back to the couch for a good long nap? Maybe.

Or it might be time to sign up for the next one.

You've stuck with your training for two months and saw what consistency and positive self-talk can do for you. I suspect other people have noticed the changes in you as well. It feels good to set your sights on a goal, chase it down and conquer it, doesn't it?

By making a commitment to yourself, sticking with it even when it's difficult, and seeing it through to the end, you've proven to yourself that you can do hard things. That you are not lazy, unmotivated, or too fat to run.

My wish for you right now is to harness that feeling and keep the momentum going. This is the time when many people feel invincible, like there is nothing that could possibly stand in their way, and after a few rest days they're going to get right back at it, becoming even stronger and faster.

And that, my friend, is a slippery slope.

If you've read my first book, *Running With Curves*, you know that's exactly what I did after my first 5K. I took a day to rest, then another for good measure. Somehow, two days turned into over two years. And I had to start all over again. So frustrating.

That's not to say you shouldn't take a couple of days to recover after a big race, but as we discussed in Week 7, a brand new running habit needs to be properly nurtured or it will wither and die. Setting your sights on another running goal is a great way to ensure you'll keep going. Here are some options:

- Train for another 5K.

- Set a time goal (aim for around a 5% improvement, so if you did your first race in 45 minutes, aim to do the next in 42:30).

- Train for a longer distance.

- Plan a "Run-Cation" around a race in an exotic location.

- Start incorporating hill repeats, sprint workouts and other drills into your workouts.

- Join the Not Your Average Runner online running group! It's totally free, **and you can sign up** at www. notyouraveragerunner.com/jointhecommunity. After you send your request to join, someone from our welcome committee will approve your request and help you settle in within a few days!

- Join an in-person running group (or start your own).

- Join a mileage challenge, e.g. 100 miles in a month, or 2000 miles in a year.

- Sign up to run a marathon with a relay team.

- Train for a sprint triathlon.

- Take a running class or clinic to help you work on form and speed.

As a special thank you for reading, I'd love to offer you a gift! Use the code 5KBOOK for a 10% discount on any Not Your Average Runner coaching programs or retreats—including the 5K 8-week online course that will help you put this book into practice!

Visit www.NotYourAverageRunner.com to learn more.

That's it, my friend! I hope you enjoyed *Not Your Average 5K* and learned the skills to continue as a runner for many years. I'd love to hear how things are going for you. If you'd like to get in touch, I can be reached at Jill@ NotYourAverageRunner.com.

And, don't forget that reward you promised yourself in Week 1!

ABOUT THE AUTHOR

Jill Angie is a certified running coach and personal trainer who wants to live in a world where everyone is free to feel fit and fabulous at any size. She started the Not Your Average Runner movement in 2013 to show that runners come in all shapes, sizes and speeds, and since then has assembled a global community of revolutionaries that are taking the running world by storm. If you would like to be part of the revolution, visit www.NotYourAverageRunner.com to find out more!

SPECIAL OFFER FOR READERS

As a special thank you for reading, I'd love to offer you a gift! Use the code 5KBOOK for a 10% discount on any Not Your Average Runner group or individual coaching programs or retreats—including the 5K 8-week online course that will help you put this book into practice!

Visit www.NotYourAverageRunner.com to learn more.

That's it, my friend! I hope you enjoyed *Not Your Average 5K* and learned the skills to continue as a runner for many years. I'd love to hear how things are going for you. If you'd like to get in touch, I can be reached at Jill@NotYourAverageRunner.com.

difference press

Difference Press offers solopreneurs, including life coaches, healers, consultants, and community leaders, a comprehensive solution to get their books written, published, and promoted. A boutique-style alternative to self-publishing, Difference Press boasts a fair and easy-to-understand profit structure, low-priced author copies, and author-friendly contract terms. Its founder, Dr. Angela Lauria, has been bringing to life the literary ventures of hundreds of authors-in-transformation since 1994.

LET'S START A MOVEMENT WITH YOUR MESSAGE

You've seen other people make a difference with a book. Now it's your turn. If you are ready to stop watching and start taking massive action. Reach out.

"Yes, I'm ready!"

In a market where hundreds of thousands books are published every year and are never heard from again, all participants of The Author Incubator have bestsellers that are actively changing lives and making a difference.

In less than two years we've created over 100 bestselling books in a row, 90% from first-time authors. As a result, our regular book programs are selling out in advance and we are selecting only the highest quality and highest potential applicants for our future programs.

Our program doesn't just teach you how to write a book—our team of coaches, developmental editors, copy editors, art directors, and marketing experts incubate you from book idea to published bestseller, ensuring that the book you create can actually make a difference in the world. We only work with the people who will use their book to get out there and make that difference.

If you have life-or world-changing ideas or services, a servant's heart, and the willingness to do what it REALLY takes to make a difference in the world with your book, go to http://theAuthorIncubator.com/apply to complete an application for the program today.

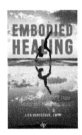
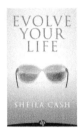

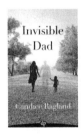

*The Unfair Affair:
How to Strengthen
and Save Your
Marriage, or Move
on with Confidence,
After Infidelity*

by Wendy Kay

*Untame Yourself:
Reconnect to the
Lost Art, Power
and Freedom of
Being a Woman*

by Elizabeth DiAlto

*Unveiling Lyme
Disease: Is
This What's
Behind Your
Chronic Illness?*

by Lisa Dennys

*Waking Up With
Dogs: Beginning
at the End*

by Melissa Courtney

*Whoops! I Forgot
To Achieve My
Potential: Create
Your Very Own
Personal Change
Management
Strategy to Get the...*

by Maggie Huffman

*Personal Finance
That Doesn't Suck: A
5-step Guide to Quit
Budgeting, Start
Wealth Building and
Get the Most from...*

by Mindy Crary

*Good Baby, Bad
Sleeper: Discover
Your Child's Sleep
Personality To
Finally Get the
Sleep You Need*

by Stephanie
Hope Dodd

*How You Can Be
with His ADHD:
What You Can
Do To Rescue Your
Relationship When
Your Partner Has
Adult ADHD*

by Mark Julian